The Dance Dragon
*One Man's [Reluctant] Journey into the
World of Ballroom Dance*

Dan Logan

First Edition Design Publishing
Sarasota, Florida USA

The Dance Dragon
Copyright ©2017 Dan Logan

ISBN 978-1506-904-35-1 HC/JAC
ISBN 978-1506-904-36-8 PBK
ISBN 978-1506-904-37-5 EBOOK

LCCN 2017943608

May 2017

Published and Distributed by
First Edition Design Publishing, Inc.
P.O. Box 20217, Sarasota, FL 34276-3217
www.firsteditiondesignpublishing.com

For Andy, Kathleen and all my friends who are dancing in the white clouds

Preface

This is a story about amateur ballroom dance, the people I met in that world, and the positive impact both have had on my life. I never imagined I would be dancing five years after my first lesson, nor did I ever envision I would write a dance story. Most of my life I avoided dance. I believed I had no rhythm and the few times I ventured onto the dance floor I felt let like a fool. I do not remember anyone disagreeing with either assessment. But when my daughter announced she was getting married, I decided to challenge my beliefs. I found an instructor, took a few dance lessons, danced at her wedding and experienced rare and random moments of joy. I needed to understand why I felt as I did and how to experience the joy of dance more often.

As a storyteller, I have tried to see myself as both an accurate reporter of, and a participant in, the ballroom dance world. At first I resisted the idea of sharing my own dance experiences, preferring to just be a reporter. In time, I felt that was a bail out on all those ballroom dancers who have shared their candid thoughts with me. My hope is that my words and the people I have introduced to the reader in this story adequately reflect the broader world of ballroom dancing and the joy that it provides.

Books do not just happen. I started four years ago with a blank page, no experience, and no idea of the effort that writing and publishing a book would take. Storytelling is a highly collaborative process that requires reaching out to people with first-hand subject matter experience as well as draft chapter readers, editors, writers, designers, publishers, social media gurus, bloggers, and on-line and traditional bookstores.

When I began my writer's journey, I enrolled in several workshops at Grub Street, a creative writing center in Boston. Every week, I listened as my fellow students read five page drafts of their memoirs and non-fiction novels. Their honesty and courage inspired me to dig deeper into my own thoughts and feelings and for that I am forever grateful. From the teachers, coaches, and consultants at Grub Street, I discovered the basics about storytelling, character development, finding my own true voice, and managing my expectations. Looking back I now know that writers and dancers share an appreciation for struggle as well as the joy and freedom that comes when you can express your own thoughts and feelings to others.

While writing, I kept numerous books on my desk and referred to them often. I was constantly reminded of the impact writers have on all our lives. The work of Kapka Kassabova in *Twelve Minutes of Love,* Steven Pressfield in *The Authentic Swing,* and Vivian Gornick's in *The Odd Woman and the City* showed me that writing non-fiction is very much about discovering oneself, trusting your inner voice, and going wherever the story takes you.

There would be no story without the people both mentioned in this book and those dancers and instructors that are not. For everyone in the story thank you for being a character and sharing your dance life with me. For those not mentioned, the depth of my appreciation is comparable. Our conversations, the effort each of you made to learn, and your shared joy of dance helped to form my perspective. These dancers and instructors, among others, include Chris, Tony, Eric, Wes, Mike, Nick, Bob, Marc, Theresa, Juanita, Marla, Kim, Chrissy, Sarah, Lisa, Paul and Jen. In addition, special thanks to every woman I have danced with for their patience as my dance partner.

Credit for this book also goes to the individuals who read my chapter drafts and challenged me to do better. People from the dance world included Xiomara Corrales, Mike Dominy, Melissa Freibe, Morgan Laskey, and Kristen Belcher. From the non -dance world I reached out to people who have known me for a long time and enjoy stories including Rick Cohn, Allison Flett, Kevin McGuinness, Ann Hughes, Lee Spelke, Jane Hitch, Nick de Sherbinin, and Shelia Murphy. Many thanks to my editor and coach Darla Bruno, my multi-tasking marketing, social media, technology and writing consultant guru Rebecca McGilloway, my son Tim Logan the journalist, for his thoughts on storytelling and editing, my daughter Caroline the one-time ballerina for first introducing me to dance as a spectator and later giving me the reason to dip my toe into the ballroom dance experience and my wife Eileen, for her unwavering support and the many roles she has played over the last four years. Writing a book requires that the author be selfish with their time and no one experienced the consequences of that more than Eileen.

You discover who you are as you go along

Steven Pressfield

Table of Contents

Chapter One

Blame it on Caroline

Blame it on my daughter, Caroline. She decided to get married, and I needed to play the role of father of the bride. I wanted to learn just one dance for the wedding, but I had a problem. There was a Dance Dragon in my head. As a child, I had always enjoyed geography and history. When I looked at old maps of the world I often noticed fierce-looking dragons. I was told dragons were drawn on maps to represent the unknown. This meant danger, a universal "do-not-enter" sign. There were some unknowns that I feared and dance was one of them. When I was young and in a situation where I was required to move my body to music, a dragon often appeared, in my head, or in the form of a shadow.

As a boy, I thought about courageous explorers like Magellan, Columbus and Marco Polo, who had to travel past the dragons on their maps into the unknown. There were times when I, too, was required to pass dragons. I was fearful of going away to college, joining the military, and living in Asia. When I passed the dragon in those situations, I was often surprised at what I came to discover; on other occasions, such as attending a funeral or speaking up in class, the dragons were optional. Sometimes I dodged those fears by taking a different path, but eventually I decided to deal with most of them. Dance was one of the few things I had managed to avoid most of my life. The problem was, the more I stayed away, the bigger the Dance Dragon became.

With Caroline getting married, I no longer had the option to avoid the Dance Dragon. Even if it was only for one dance, I had to face it. I thought about all the weddings I had attended and the number of times I had watched fathers make fools of themselves on the dance floor. That was not going to be my fate. I wondered how many of those men also had a Dance Dragon in their head. My plan was simple. I would find an instructor to prepare myself for the encounter, focus on my one dance goal and, if necessary, face the dragon. I would surprise my daughter and my wife, Eileen, with my dancing skill at the wedding and then return to my happy, dance-free life. Little did I know that I would meet Melissa, an instructor, have a different dance experience at my daughter's wedding than expected, dance with more than 3,000 women within a few years, travel to rural Cuba in search of the feel of the dance, and rumba at a competitive ballroom dance event in front of hundreds of people in Washington D. C.

As a child, I seldom heard music playing in our house and never saw anyone dance. We were five boys, two parents and a dog. Ours was not a big house: four small bedrooms and a bathroom upstairs, a kitchen, living room, dining room and half-bath downstairs. An unfinished basement served as the laundry room. If we children were not eating, sleeping, doing homework, or sick, we were sent outdoors, along with the dog, to play. My mother liked a quiet house. Music and dancing were simply not part of our daily lives. That was fine with me. I liked sports.

My mother always said she was blessed to have five sons. I was number four. Sometimes I asked myself if she truly meant that, or whether she was simply rationalizing her fate, or "God's will," as she would describe it. As a young man, I speculated whether my social skills and comfort level with music, dance, and girls might have been different if I'd had a sister.

With neither the desire nor the skill, my mother never even attempted to be a good housekeeper. She insisted from the time we could walk that we make our own beds, clean our rooms, and be well-dressed for school, church, and extended family gatherings. We always washed our hands when we came into the house, kept our elbows off the table at dinner, and said "please "and "thank you", though little else, when adults were present. I never danced with my mother, nor do I recollect ever seeing her dance. I sensed that if I suddenly asked my mother to dance with me or started moving my body to music, she might panic and call the doctor or, even worse, the priest.

My father was a work machine, often balancing several jobs: liquor salesman, owner of a seaside snack bar and then a liquor store. When he was at home, which was rarely, he was fixing our well-traveled cars, unclogging a sink or toilet, painting a room, or working in the yard. If you were within his sight, you were recruited to help. Participation was not optional. For recreation, he would listen to the Red Sox game on the radio. I never heard him listen to music or saw him dance. Once or twice a year, he would take me to Fenway Park. Baseball was my first passion in sports, followed by Notre Dame football. I was by far the most intense sports fan of his five sons, and he and I bonded over that. We never discussed dancing, nor girls, for that matter. His most precious gift to me was teaching me that I should always help, respect, and love my mother.

The first time I encountered the Dance Dragon was in my junior year in high school. The auditorium was warm. The industrial lights were bright and hot. We had come to Newton Country Day School, an all-girl Catholic school that was the sister school to my all-boy high school. It was the third Friday in October and that meant the first obligatory dance lesson and party for the young gentlemen in my class. If we did not attend, the school would call our parents - there were no exceptions. As young gentlemen, it was assumed we would all want to know how to dance. There would be proms and cotillions in our future, or so we were told.

As I walked into the auditorium with my friends, in my tweed sports jacket, heavy wool pants, white button-down shirt, and red-and-black-striped school tie, I thought about the six pimples that I had counted on my face that morning, and the fresh two-inch-long razor cut on my chin from trying to get rid of my peach fuzz that morning. My hands were sweaty.

The boys were told to line up opposite the girls, then walk across the floor and ask a young lady to dance. We practiced asking the girl several times until we got it right. After a few dances, we paused while a humorless middle-aged woman demonstrated how the boys, and then the girls, should dance. She instructed us on the art of social conversation. My feeble attempts to follow her suggestions with my dance partners sounded phony to me. I rebelled at the idea of saying nice things to people whom I neither knew nor cared about. Beads of sweat bubbled up on my forehead each time I crossed the dance floor. The only dance I could remember was the waltz. I watched my heavy black shoes move in a square box until the music ended.

At that age, dancing was complicated and contradictory. As gentlemen, we were supposed to hold the girl's right hand with our left hand while we placed our right hand on her upper back. We would then move our feet to the music in the desired direction but never think about or have contact with any other female body part. That was forbidden. To avoid the risk of inappropriate physical contact, I kept the middle of my body as far away from my partner as possible. My friends and I referred to this as the "banana pose". My hips and butt were so far back from my partner that my body was curved like a banana. My body was so tense when I danced that my back ached. The bodies I danced with came in a variety of sizes and shapes. The bigger the body, the more difficult it was to maintain my distance. To make matters worse, my dance partners and I were often clumsy. Physical contact with my partner was an accident waiting to happen. It was merely a question of when, with whom, and how she would react. I hated everything that I was doing and kept looking at the clock on the wall. Someday, I kept telling myself, someday, I would be free.

After an hour of sweat and pain, the sequence changed. Things got worse. The instructor had the girls walk toward the boys and ask us for a dance. I saw her walking toward me. She was a big girl with a wide forehead, red hair, a very plain flat face, and a false smile. I weighed maybe 150 pounds, was five-foot-eight, and was shorter than this girl in her dance shoes. This was not the girl of my dreams. She was going to ask me to dance, and there was no escape. "May I have this dance?" she asked.

I lied and told her I would be happy to dance. I put my wet left hand out and connected with her dry hand, took a deep breath, released my peppermint-scented breath, and started to walk the waltz. Her name was Mary, and she immediately started to practice the art of conversation. "Are you having a good time?" Mary asked. I decided to be honest.

I told Mary it was too warm in the room, dancing was not my favorite activity, and I would rather be somewhere else. What I did not say to Mary was that sweat was running down my arms and legs, and my lower back was in constant pain. I did not mention my dislike of the chaperones watching us with their foolish smiles, for fear that one of them was her parent. I had the mindset of a rebellious teenager counting the days to my freedom. I assumed she wanted to grow up and be just like her parents.

Mary told me that I was not dancing correctly. I should stand straight up, close to her but be careful not to step on her feet. *Wow, things were getting risky*, I thought. I told Mary I would do my best, but that I didn't know how to dance. As we started dancing again, a boy bumped Mary's back and pushed her towards me. I managed to pull back just in time and no contact was made. Mary was not happy. She told me she wished boys would watch where they are going. I said nothing but gave a slight nod.

Mary asked me if I had a girlfriend. I was surprised at her question. This was not the social conversation skill we'd been taught. Again, I was honest. "Mary, I don't date. With sports, I never get home until suppertime and then I need to do homework for three hours every night. On the weekends, except in the summer, I work at my father's liquor store. At an all-boy school, there are no girls to meet. " She smiled.

The music stopped and, as I lowered my left hand, the unthinkable happened. It brushed against Mary's breast. My mouth opened to apologize, but no words came out. I looked away, rolled my eyes, and waited for her reaction. I could feel my heart pumping. I caught the look of panic on her face, or was it anger? Mary said nothing as she quickly walked away. I assumed she saw me as a groper or worse, and my behavior would be reported to a dance chaperone. By the end of the evening, every girl in the dance hall would think I was a pervert.

I escaped to the men's room. I lit the first of two Lucky Strike cigarettes I'd tucked away, inhaled, and thought about what had just happened. At some point, I would have to go back out there. Would Mary and the dance police be waiting for me? Would I be reported to the priests at my school or to my parents? The whole thing was an accident, but who would trust the motives of a teenage boy? This never would have happened if I did not have to take dance lessons. I took a few deep breaths, flushed my second cigarette down the toilet, and washed my hands in the sink. I looked at my pale, sweaty face in the mirror with the red pimples and the razor cut, both of which seemed bigger than before. What a mess.

I opened the door and started walking, on shaky legs. I was trying to prepare myself for either the dance police or another dance, unsure which was worse. No one appeared to be waiting for me. I felt dizzy, there was a foul smell in the air, and then I saw him. A large dragon, maybe eight feet tall, was standing on the edge of the dance floor. He had red eyes and green scales over most of his body, and he was looking right at me. I started to back away from the dance floor. A male chaperone found me, asked me if I was okay, and then led me to a girl who needed a partner. The rest of the party was a blur.

A year later, I had my second dragon sighting. It was October, and I was a senior in high school. I was studying in my room when my mother knocked on my door and told me there was a girl on the phone asking for me. She did not mention her name. What! Who could it be? I asked myself. I only knew a few girls and they would never call me at home. This had never happened before. I felt my freckled face turn red. I went downstairs to the living room, picked up the phone and said hello. My parents appeared to be reading the evening paper, but I knew they were all ears. There was no privacy in my house. This was an awful situation. "Hi Dan, this is Karen. How are things with you?"

I knew Karen from North Scituate beach where my family rented a cottage every summer. Karen was not part of my crowd. She had blond hair, a small frame, and a pleasant smile. I was polite and told Karen that I was busy with school and filling out college applications. Karen asked if I was doing anything on December 18th, and if not, would I like to come to a cotillion dance in Boston and be one of her escorts?

I felt faint. My mind turned to mush and then memories of the Dance Dragon flashed before my eyes. I would rather visit hell for an evening than go to a cotillion. Of course, I was free on December 18th, it was two months off. My parents were sitting less than twenty feet away. I could not lie with them in the room. I was desperate to be truthful and say no but I knew my mother would tell me that answer was selfish and hurtful. Plus, unlike my three older brothers, I had never officially dated a girl or brought one home to meet the family. I kept that part of my life private. Such behavior made my parents curious. I lied to Karen and said I would enjoy coming. When I hung up the phone, my mother looked at me and noticed my red face was now pale. After some explanation, she was happy that I had said yes.

The person Karen thought she had invited to her cotillion that night was a senior at St. Sebastian's Country Day School for young gentlemen. The problem was I had a split personality in those days. There was another Dan, the one who was not interested in being a young gentleman, in the academic and social standing of his high school, or in going to a dance. The first Dan had attended Catholic elementary school, served as an altar boy, and excelled in religion class. The prevalent thinking among his parents and the nuns from his school was that a strict all boys' Catholic high school, as opposed to a co-ed public school, would keep his faith strong. At the time, it was a commonly held belief that Catholic teenage boys needed strong faith to avoid the temptations of sin, which was code for "girls". To Karen's family, the first Dan appeared to be a fine young Catholic gentleman, based on his resume.

December 18th arrived. The ball was the social coming-out night of the year for Irish Catholic young ladies of Boston. I had rented a tuxedo and looked handsome, or so my mother said as I left the house. The air was cold as I walked towards the ballroom in the Park Plaza hotel but I knew inside I would be hot, sweaty, and uncomfortable. My primary goal for the evening was to do the obligatory dance with Karen, though I had no idea how to do it. My second goal was to be on my best behavior and not to make a fool of myself. If I could achieve those two goals, I told myself, my reward would be that I would never have to agree to attend a dance party again. Before walking into the ballroom, I visited some of my male friends upstairs in a hotel room and had two beers. I was very disciplined.

When I arrived at the table, the reception was cool, though I was not sure why. I had received a formal invitation in the mail but no other details or instructions. Karen was quite pleasant, but her family and friends—none of whom I knew—were aloof. Perhaps I had not lived up to the build-up or had missed an earlier activity. Perhaps my attempts at social conversation were inept or they sensed I had stopped for a beer. I didn't ask. After 15 minutes, I assumed I must have been unwittingly disrespectful of Karen's family or breached some unwritten protocol, and there was no recovery. I excused myself and went for a long walk in the cold winter air. I was not happy with myself. I decided I must return and ask Karen to dance.

I returned to the ballroom and looked for Karen, but instead I saw the Dance Dragon's shadow on the dance floor. He was bigger than the last time, particularly his head. Among his teeth were two large fangs, which I had not noticed before. My legs felt like Jell-O and I could hear my heartbeat. I stopped looking for Karen, drifted towards the back of the room, and escaped from the building. I was a coward. On the drive home, I promised myself that never again would I put myself in such a situation. I would leave Boston and the social life others had planned for me and start a fresh life, a life that did not require dancing.

Chapter Two

The Instructor

Caroline's wedding was in August, just four months away. How was I going to learn to dance? Who could I ask for advice? Where could I go? The clock was ticking. I had no male friends or family members who took dance seriously. My friend Hank, after a few glasses of wine, enjoyed dancing the Peabody with my wife, Eileen, but that dance was popular when Woodrow Wilson was president. Kevin, a close friend since college, was not a bad dancer, but he lived in Michigan. Plus, asking another guy to teach me to dance seemed weird. I thought about women I knew who could dance, and that was a short list. I also realized it would be complicated. How would I approach a woman and ask her to teach me to dance but not to tell my wife or daughter?

I could ask Eileen to teach me or help me find an instructor. But that presented another set of challenges. Music and dance were part of her everyday life growing up. She was the youngest of four, loved to dance, and often danced with her siblings and their friends. Eileen's nieces and nephews enjoyed dancing, and at family weddings I would always be the odd one out who avoided the dance floor. A few times in the past Eileen had tried to teach me a dance step or two, with no luck. While she was a very competent dancer, I doubted she had the patience to be my teacher. After thirty-five years of marriage, asking Eileen to teach me to dance might drive her over the edge. She had plenty on her mind with the wedding. Dancing at my daughter's wedding was my challenge, and I alone needed to find a solution.

I conducted my search for a professional instructor in a clandestine manner. I saw no need to discuss the dragon with anyone; after all, I had kept his existence a secret all my life. I visited the websites of dance studios that were close by. Location was important as lessons would require that I be "missing in action" for an hour or two each week. A squash match or a client lunch would make a good cover story.

My office was located on Canal Street near the Boston Garden, a seedy neighborhood in transition. The first place I found online was just two blocks away. I assumed I could drop by the studio at lunchtime for lessons, and no one in my office would notice any change in my behavior. I had no intention of announcing my need to take dance lessons to my work associates. The reaction would have been shock and disbelief followed by laughter as soon as I left the room.

I read on the website that the studio has been in business for more than thirty years. If so, the owner's photograph must have been taken years ago. I scrolled down to the class section. They offered street funk, hip-hop and jazz, but there was no mention of weddings. I moved on.

Another studio, located seven miles away, welcomed beginners, taught ballroom dancing, and had a focus on weddings. The owner was born in Minsk, Russia, and trained by several accomplished Russian dancers. I thought about Caroline's twelve years at the Boston Ballet and the Russian instructors she had worked with. They were great dancers, but she never described them as sensitive or patient. I tried to envision my first conversation with this man. He looked a bit like Vladimir Putin. Would I tell him I had no rhythm or that I was uncomfortable learning to move my body to music in front of others? I hesitated. This was not the answer.

I clicked on the Arthur Murray studio. It was convenient, just 15 minutes from my office, and had afternoon classes. I had vague recollections of Arthur Murray himself from the early days of television. I assumed he must be either dead or close to one hundred years old. The website was not that informative. It provided no resumes or photos of the instructors and was highly promotional. I was suspicious. Why would they not have photographs of the instructors? What were they trying to hide? The location of the studio, in Boston's Park Plaza building, brought back unpleasant memories of that cotillion night and my dragon sighting decades ago. It sent a cold chill through me.

Whichever studio I chose, I knew I would walk in looking like a lost tourist, a sucker who had just arrived in the big city. I needed to be able to evaluate the people and chemistry quickly and avoid the hard sell. I had to know what I was looking for in an instructor and make sure I had an exit strategy. The budget I had in my head was five hundred dollars. In exchange for my money, I sought competency in a single dance. The price seemed high but it was worth it.

The elevator stopped on the third floor. I located the door for the Arthur Murray studio. The air in the hallway was stale but it was not foul. I took a deep breath, both to relax and to see if I smelled anything resembling a dragon. My left hand reached for the doorknob, and I slowly opened the door. The receptionist asked me to take a seat. A few minutes later, a young woman named Kristen introduced herself and shook my hand. She owned the voice on the phone and knew why I was there. Kristen was responsible for new students and got right to the point. I was to dance with an instructor, Melissa, and then we would talk and determine if she was the right instructor for me.

A tall woman with long arms walked across the room toward me. She held her head up and shoulders back as she approached. Melissa was not what I had expected. Melissa had blue eyes, blond/reddish hair, and a wrinkle-free face and looked me right in the eyes when she spoke. Caroline, my daughter, was almost as tall, with blue eyes, similar hair color and a soft voice. A coincidence? After we exchanged pleasantries Melissa said, "Let's dance, Dan. " With those three words, my journey began.

I was no more qualified to evaluate a dance instructor than to pass judgment on a midwife. My favorite coaches or mentors in the past were likeable people whom I respected for their work ethic and with whom I felt I could be honest. But in those situations, I knew enough about the subject, be it tennis, golf, squash, or skiing, to realize they were competent at what they did. They were also highly regarded by my peers. This time was different. I knew nothing about dance and no one had recommended Melissa or the studio. Dance was also unusual in that it almost instantly required physical intimacy with a total stranger, a person of the opposite sex. Dance was unlike any sport I had ever experienced.

I did not see Melissa's resume. I wondered how often this young woman had succeeded at teaching men like me to dance. I decided not to ask Melissa any tough questions. She was working hard at being nice, plus I was not interviewing her for a heart transplant operation. In time, I would learn that Melissa was relatively new as an instructor. She did not try to sell herself to me, but she did take over the conversation. She asked questions about my background and expectations.

As we talked and danced, I kept my distance, my shoulders hunched, and occasionally watched my feet move in a square box. I felt awkward. On the dance floor, I lacked the confidence I felt in sports, business, and other aspects of life. Was I ready to embarrass myself in front of this young woman and other dancers in the studio? I could still abandon my plan; Caroline and Eileen would never know.

Melissa asked what type of dance I might do at the wedding. I explained that I was not that familiar with the names of different dances or what they involved. I was vaguely aware of the waltz, the hustle, and the tango from watching movies. Melissa moved on to Caroline and her dance preferences. I mentioned I didn't know what Caroline liked to dance as we never danced together. Plus, I had planned to surprise her. We moved on to talk about possible wedding songs, but I had no idea about that either.

In hindsight, Melissa must have thought when it came to dance I was one amazingly naïve man. She let me know that she thought it great that I wanted to surprise Caroline but, given the timeline, we might want to settle on a song and a dance as a starting point so we could practice. Melissa suggested that I might consider the foxtrot, the rumba, or the foxy as wedding dances. As we talked, I realized my original plan had not been well thought-out. I felt like I was the patient on the couch and Melissa, with her soft voice, was the sympathetic listener. She asked good questions without making me feel like a fool. She let me draw my own conclusions.

Melissa grew up in Minnesota, went to high school in rural Nebraska, left home after college, and had come more than 1,500 miles to Boston to start her career. At seventeen, I did something of the reverse. I left Boston to escape from everything I knew and traveled 1,000 miles to the Midwest. Both my children would also leave Boston and go to the Midwest for college. Melissa's mother was a teacher who liked music and theatre. Melissa told me she hadn't spent much time dancing as a child. When she moved to Boston, she planned to pursue a career in photography. Only then did she stumble into dance, and it took over her life.

After 20 minutes, I decided Melissa would be my instructor. The location was an advantage, and I was comfortable talking to her. She had a nice mix of energy, passion, and patience to deal with someone as clueless as me. If I had to make a fool of myself in front of an instructor, Melissa seemed liked a good choice. I found her genuine. The downside was my nervousness at the thought of dancing with someone who was so graceful and elegant on the dance floor. I told myself I would just have to get over that. I signed up for five lessons and felt good about my decision. Melissa gave me a questionnaire to complete as homework.

The questionnaire listed fifteen possible benefits I could derive from dance. My task was to rank the top five based on importance. I was only interested in one: making a special person happy. That was why I walked in the studio door. The rest of the form felt like filling out a questionnaire for a used-car salesman before the one-on-one session. The more I exposed myself, the easier it became for the person offering the service to find a problem to solve. But rather than be blunt with Melissa and say I just wanted to learn one dance for a wedding, I decided to play nice and risk putting myself in harm's way. I was strong enough to resist her sales pitch, and I needed to build a relationship, and trust Melissa to prepare me for my wedding dance. Getting the questionnaire completed was part of her job, and I did not want to make that job any more difficult.

The second benefit that I checked off was that I wanted to never again say "no" to someone who asked me to dance. Too often I had declined dance requests. I assumed most females, be they relative, friend, or stranger, who asked a male to dance, enjoyed dancing and that I should try to say yes. I realized that saying no was a selfish act and, at times, it bothered me. However, it bothered me less than facing the dragon.

My third reason was to reduce shyness and self-consciousness on the dance floor. The day I walked in the door I felt awkward dancing with

Melissa and was reminded of one reason I did not dance. If a person does not know how to move their body the right way, whether skiing, playing squash, or dancing, they become over-sensitive and tense. In dance, I needed to be physically close to my partner and lead her by moving my body to the music. I was an embarrassment waiting to happen. This, I knew, could not be overcome in five lessons.

Distant fourth and fifth reasons were to pursue more fun in my social life with Eileen and acquire social ease on the dance floor. Most people who know me would say I'm at ease with almost any social group and I have my share of fun. However, if I were asked what created a sense of discomfort for me socially, dancing would be on my list. Whenever Eileen and I were asked to an event with dancing, I was quick to find a way to say no, though Eileen would probably have enjoyed it. At a wedding, I could usually be found lurking in the background when dance time came. I left the completed form at the front desk for Melissa.

Melissa was well-organized. I wondered where she got her energy and how long she could sustain her positive attitude with me. I was more accustomed to the drill-sergeant teaching approach that I experienced in the military, in school, and in sports. Before our lesson, Melissa thanked me for completing the questionnaire and said it would help her to know my goals. She hoped that I would keep taking lessons until I reached the point where I did not feel the need to say no to dancing with anyone. I listened to her, smiled, and nodded. Melissa was sincere and believed what she said. She was unusual that way. She was also clever. She had dropped a hint about a long-term goal, but I didn't take the bait. I was only interested in the wedding dance.

Melissa introduced me to the foxy, which was the wedding dance she recommended for Caroline and me. She reminded me that we could always change our minds. She described it as a simple slow-travel dance derived from the foxtrot. Of course, it was not simple for me. As we started to practice, I kept my distance from Melissa to avoid accidental body contact with someone I hardly knew. I had no idea of the etiquette of a ballroom dance studio. I found it amusing that Melissa was long and I was short. We were opposites in so many ways. When I tried my first over arm turn I stood on my tiptoes and raised Melissa's arm over her head. I was clumsy, and I lost my balance. Melissa let me know if I stopped backing away and stood closer to her, I would find dancing easier.

I laughed to myself. I wondered what Melissa thought of me standing so far away from her. In time, she would teach me how to read non-verbal messages from my dance partners as to their preferred distance. The decision, she said should be my partner's, not mine. At studio dance parties, I would later experience my first chest bumps and learn how to deal with them on my own.

The next time I danced with Melissa, I took a double lesson. We had a lot of work to do, she explained, and I agreed. I soon realized that, as an employee of a dance studio, optimizing billable hours was part of her job. In fairness to Melissa, predicting how many lessons it might take me to learn a dance was impossible. The balancing act between the benefit of lessons and their cost was often on my mind. However, the priority in my head was mastering the basics of my dance.

Melissa did not have an easy job with me. She had to dumb down basic concepts. She pointed out how I should use my arm to escort Caroline on and off the dance floor. She would take my hand and tap on it with her fingers so I could get a sense of the beat. When my dance steps were too big, she would bend down on the floor and move my feet so that I got a sense of distance and balance. We would talk about leading with the left heel on the first step of the foxy and shifting my weight without moving my feet. I seldom got things right the first or the second time; it was slow going. I marveled at the extent of Melissa's patience.

After my fourth lesson, I knew my original plan of taking five dance lessons and surprising Caroline at her wedding with my dance skill was seriously flawed. The plan must be revised. I needed more private lessons and to involve Eileen, so I could practice with her at home. I also wanted to get a sense of how important this dance was to Caroline, and her thoughts on what song and the type of dance she would like. She might have a different set of expectations. I realized no one knew I had been taking lessons or anything about the dragon. Since it was late June and the wedding wasn't until August, I could still abort the entire plan.

Chapter Three

The Wedding Dance

My daughter Caroline had always been my window to the world of little girls and dance. As a girl, she loved to figure-skate, practiced ballet for years and later, in college, performed modern dance. She enjoyed costumes; make up, dressing-room gossip, and performing. I remembered a rainy Saturday afternoon when I first witnessed the joy little girls got from dancing. I had taken a break from my work, heard the music, and walked back to the den. Caroline and several of her friends were dancing on the coffee table with their socks on. One of our favorite movies, *Dirty Dancing,* was playing on the VCR. My arrival was noticed but did not change their behavior. The girls were singing, "*Be My Baby*" by the Ronettes. The girls held pretend microphones in their hands and wiggled their hips to the beat of the music in the fun-filled room. *Dirty Dancing* features Jennifer Grey as "Baby," a teenage girl who falls in love with Johnny Castle, the dance instructor (played by Patrick Swayze), at a resort in the Catskills. The girls told me that only a few men in the world could dance like Patrick Swayze. Some fathers would have danced with these little girls right on the spot, but not me. I remained on the sidelines. I loved the music, the dance scenes in the movie, and watching my daughter and her friends have fun. But there was no way I was going to make a fool out of myself.

As the years went by, Caroline dreamed about joining a ballet company. I saw her deal with frustration, chronic back pain, mangled toes, and the sad departure of many of her friends from the ballet program. Ballet is physically demanding, mentally tough and, for a teenage girl on a professional track, close to a full-time job. But Caroline pursued her dream, stayed focused and worked hard. She spent her summers attending ballet programs in Ohio, Florida, and London. As we traveled to and from such places, I would listen to her concerns, hear about the dance people she met, and try to imagine what life as a professional ballerina might be like. The competition for advancement kept getting tougher. Her life in ballet introduced me to a world that I hadn't known, and my respect for dancers grew. I came to appreciate the discipline, body control, and creative expression dance requires. I saw, close–up, the connection between music, body movement, and human emotion. It was beautiful, complicated, and beyond me. I became a fan of dance, but not a dancer.

The stereotypical image of the father-daughter relationship portrayed in wedding movies often depicts dim-witted fathers who have a soft spot for their little girls. Too often in such scenarios, the daughter is characterized as spoiled, naïve, and unable to manage life on her own. In the real world, I had watched Caroline's friends and peers grow up. They were different from that image. They decided which college to attend, what career path to pursue, and if and whom they would marry. While I may have a soft spot for Caroline, I respected her for her work ethic, kindness to others and her desire to manage her own life. She, like other young women, had to compete in a male-dominated business world, and the games that are played in that world are not always nice. My role has never been to encourage Caroline to avoid those waters, but rather to help her navigate them successfully. She was directing and managing her own wedding, and I needed to hear her perspective on what role she wanted me to play. I sent her a text, her preferred medium, and the two of us met for dinner.

Caroline recommended we order one of her favorite craft draft beers, Peaks, an organic pilsner. She was an expert on craft beers. I inquired about her workday. Caroline told me she was very busy. She had been working for four years at Boston Medical Center in the day and going to night school at Boston University for her Master's degree in public health. Her career plan was to pursue a doctorate in Health Care Policy. Along with marriage, life was changing for her in a big way.

I decided it was time to test the waters and asked how things were going with the wedding. Everything was coming together, Caroline said, but it was an amazing amount of work to organize an outdoor wedding in Vermont, 200 miles from home. She was still trying to find low-cost places for people to stay. Their friends had to travel a long way and most of them had little money. One friend had volunteered to be the DJ for the dancing after dinner, but they were still trying to determine what to play during the wedding ceremony. Gill, her husband-to-be, and his musician friends had many ideas. I asked her thoughts about the wedding dances, and she threw the ball back at me. Like her brother Tim, Caroline had always referred to me by my first name rather than "Dad".

"Dan, what was your wedding like, what music did you play, did you dance?"

I explained that our wedding was at the U. N. chapel across the street from the United Nations and that Eileen and I wrote our own vows. We promised to support each other in life and there was no reference to the idea that a woman should be asked to obey her husband. We invited seventy-five people, as that was all we could afford for the reception. At the wedding we played three songs. We loved the Beatles and John Lennon. The lyrics of their songs captured who we were and how we both felt about life. We played *"Imagine," "Here Comes the Sun,"* and *"In My Life."*

For the reception, we invited our guests to a small bar that looked out on the U. N. We served drinks and appetizers. The space was tight, and we had no DJ. The bartender put some music on but there was no significant dancing. I reminded her that dancing was not one of my strong points.

Caroline offered no comments on my dancing. I assumed she concurred but nevertheless expected we would perform a father-daughter dance. She mentioned she liked the Beatles and the songs that we played but that it would be weird for her to choose one of her parents' wedding songs.

I agreed and suggested we might want a song that reflected a feeling, a thought, or a memorable moment that we both experienced. I also needed a song to which I could dance. Caroline, with a mischievous smile, asked what songs might fit that requirement. The moment had arrived. I was at the fork in the road. I could say I was hopeless at dancing, or mention the lessons and the foxy. Both answers would be true. I mentioned that I had been taking some dance lessons on my own, but I still had a way to go.

Caroline seemed happy and surprised. She wanted to know all the details. I recapped my visit to the studio, described Melissa, and mentioned her suggestions on the foxy and that father and daughter should take a few lessons together. I told Caroline that dance lessons were hard, and I was a fish out of water. I asked if she was familiar with the foxy. Caroline smiled but did not give a direct answer. She went dancing with her friends in Cambridge frequently, but I sensed she had no idea what the foxy was. Ballroom dancing was not her thing.

I told Caroline I had thought about the songs from *Dirty Dancing* like *The Time of My Life* or *Be My Baby* as possible wedding songs, but Patrick Swayze was a tough act for me to follow. I mentioned two songs that we played a lot as a family, Bruce Springsteen's, *Dancin' in the Dark* and *Paradise by the Dashboard Lights* by Meatloaf. Of course, both might have been strange songs for a wedding dance. "What are your favorites? What are you thinking?" I inquired.

Caroline responded that she liked the idea of the Beatles, and that their music worked at weddings, we both liked them, and had listened to them over the years. *"All You Need is Love"* she replied with confidence and excitement. "Dan, I'm glad you're taking lessons and like the idea of taking them together. It makes a lot of sense. I keep wondering about Gill and our wedding dance. He may be a musician, but he is a goofy dancer. He also needs to practice. "

On my way home, I wondered what words Caroline would use to describe my dancing. I'd been tempted to ask her earlier. However, Caroline works hard at being truthful yet sensitive, and I didn't want to put her on the spot. I liked the song *All You Need Is Love* by the Beatles. While it may have seemed a bit idealistic, I believed in the lyrics. Love is powerful, and a life without love is not a pleasant thought.

Caroline came to the studio several times for dance lessons and Melissa choreographed a foxy dance to our wedding song. The music and the song fit with who Caroline is and the mood she was trying to create.

When August arrived, Melissa started pushing me to expand my dancing experiences by attending group lessons and beginner dance parties. By now, I had taken ten private lessons. I had lost control of my budget, but I was learning more about dancing and something about myself. Melissa had a way of being persistent but not irritating. Whenever I lightheartedly grilled her on her persistency, her answer about parties and group classes made sense. Melissa would tell me she was looking after my best interests, as there would be other women at the wedding that I would want to dance with besides Eileen and Caroline. I also realized that she was hoping the more exposure I had to dance, the more likely I would return after the wedding. The group lessons were challenging and at times painful, but I stayed with them because of the support of the female partners I met. They wanted to help me learn. The culture of positive reinforcement was not limited to the instructors.

My first Wednesday night dance party at the studio was far more challenging for me than a group class. Parties were held on the main studio floor, and about thirty students and a few instructors attended. It was expected that I would dance to every song and no instructor would be counting the beat aloud for me to time my steps. My partner would be relying on me to lead the steps. That night, I focused on asking women who I recognized from my group classes to dance. We were encouraged to switch partners after each dance. I battled with my inner self, grunted a lot, and felt physically awkward and embarrassed at times. I could not remember all the steps or hand moves. My conversations were sporadic. I sensed, but did not see, the dragon lurking in the room. I found the party both mentally and emotionally exhausting.

After a dozen dances, I needed to leave, confident I could make it to the door without drawing attention to myself. I was wrong. Six steps from the door, I sensed a tall presence behind me, but it was not the Dance Dragon. It was Melissa. She did not reprimand me for my attempt at escape. That was not her style. She simply asked me to dance. I paused, then smiled and nodded in affirmation. I appreciated how clever and charming this young lady could be. Melissa knew, from the look on my face, that, like the people in a Southwest Airline commercial, "I desperately wanted to get away. "She also knew from the questionnaire that I had completed my first day that I did not want to refuse someone who asked me to dance. The battle within me lasted a few seconds and then I conceded and said yes to her. A few dances later, I left the studio ready, in my mind, for the wedding and the foxy. That Wednesday night party turned out to be a good warm-up for the wedding. Melissa did succeed in securing a commitment from me to return to the studio to tell her about the wedding dance. Of course, I had no doubt we would also talk about my interest in any future dancing. I respected her tenacity but, in my own mind, I was confident that after the wedding I would return to my old life of squash and golf, and avoiding the dance floor.

The wedding was outdoors on a Vermont farm on the edge of the Mad River. Bill and Brian, who had escaped to Vermont decades ago, owned the small farmhouse, which had breathtaking views. Caroline and Gill had stayed at the farm several times on weekend ski trips and rented the outdoor space for two days for the wedding. The view from the lawn would make for a great postcard. The river, flowers, rock gardens and majestic trees with the Green Mountains in the background made the location special. The smell of cut grass and the sound of running water from the river filled the air that late summer weekend.

The idea was to keep the wedding simple and as close to nature as possible. Although a city girl, Caroline is part-hippie and part-yogi, and appreciates the outdoors and nature. The wedding reflected the values and personality that she and Gill shared. That afternoon, nature responded well to Gill and Caroline's wishes. The next day, nature would be in a different mood.

Behind the scenes, there were some pre-wedding tense moments on the logistical front, but I assumed there always are. Caroline, with her grace and patience, set the example for all of us and never lost her cool or her sense of humor. The guests all helped with their assigned chores to make sure the day was perfect for her.

I was up at 5:30 a. m. and took Daniel, my grandson and Caroline's young nephew, for a walk, so everyone else could sleep. I always enjoyed my walks with Daniel. At 18 months, his mind was full of curiosity, and unlike adults, he focused only on the moment. I was jealous of his uncluttered mind. I never knew if, when, or where Daniel might want to stop and what he might select to examine. He was unpredictable. That morning, he decided to stop at a large statue of a dairy cow, a creature very important to the state of Vermont. He examined the cow in detail while I thought ahead through the day. I felt great for someone who had been living on four or five hours of sleep for days. Friends and family had arrived. I was prepared for the walk down the grassy slope from the farmhouse to the river's edge. The comments I would make at dinner were in my head, and I felt comfortable about the dance with Caroline. My daughter was happy and ready for marriage. I reminded myself Eileen would no longer have wedding planning nightmares, and we could rest all day Sunday.

Ten hours later, I put my arm out for Caroline to hold, and we walked down the hill. The sky was painted blue with a few fluffy white clouds and there was a cool late-afternoon August breeze. The guests sat on white chairs or stood in the shade of a few large oak trees as the musicians played. We headed for a gazebo-like setting by a narrow point on the river. I passed Caroline off to Gill and took my seat next to Eileen. My brother performed the ceremony and happiness and celebration filled the air. During the reception, several children took off their shoes and waded into the wide, shallow riverbed downstream behind the old farmhouse. As the sun fell below the mountains, we headed for the tent and dinner. Soft candlelight filled the room and spread across the tables with their apple-green runners and cream-colored table cloths. Small lights wrapped around the tent poles twinkled in the dusk. The effort made by so many people arranging the room that morning was magical.

When the time came to walk out on the dance floor and do the foxy with Caroline, I was ready. The dragon was not on my mind. I took a few deep breaths and focused only on Caroline. I started the dance with the happiest girl in Vermont. My feet moved with the music, and I kept my head up and shoulders back. Caroline smiled and there was no tension in her body. Dancing the foxy was amazingly easy as our dance reflected how we felt. The music carried us around the room. We just seemed to float. We talked about the day, how well everything had gone. I thought how about how light on her feet Caroline was, and how she just seemed to follow my lead. I had been told that is the way dancing is supposed to be.

At a wedding, the father of the bride wears a big target that reads "Ask Me to Dance". During dinner, I found time to dance, and again after dinner. I was determined not to say no regardless of the music or my dance partner. In the candlelight, I danced with friends, relatives, and people I had never met. One of Caroline's friends from college, Jackie, was a singer and jazz musician who performed in Austin, Chicago, and on occasion, the East Coast. I think she detected that I was not completely in my comfort zone. She asked me to dance and follow her lead. Jackie then did some counting to get me to slow down. After the dance, we drifted to the side, and she showed me some slow and simple body moves. Jackie had the gift of music, you could see it in the way she moved her body. Dance was instinctive to her. When I first met her as a freshman in college, Jackie told me music and baseball were her passions. I knew nothing about music so, as the years went by, I would ask her about baseball. A decade later, I found her helping me dance and I marveled at her passion for music. I reminded myself that evening that I was not in a ballroom setting, there was no right or wrong way to dance, and I needed to just go with the flow.

After a long stretch on the dance floor I took a break, grabbed a beer, and went for a walk around the farm. I thought about the guests. Gill's parents were born in Bulgaria and now lived in Westchester County, New York. His friends and family had traveled from places like South Africa, France, and New Zealand, as well as New York. Caroline's friends came mostly from Iowa, Texas, Illinois, Wisconsin, the New York City area and Boston. Dancing seemed to be a common thread that helped bring this eclectic bunch together. When I returned to the tent, I came across my niece, Leanne. She is the daughter of Eileen's sister, and, like everyone in Eileen's family, she loved to dance. Leanne was the working mother of two young children and the wedding was a chance for her family to come to Vermont for a vacation. I had been to numerous weddings on Eileen's side of the family and decided to end my multi-decade long danceless streak with her family. I asked Leanne to dance and returned to the dance floor.

Jessie, the DJ, had done an awesome job of mixing up the music so there was something that appealed to everyone. He had just finished playing one of my favorite songs *"All Night Long"* by Lionel Richie. As Leanne and I approached the open area to dance, Jesse announced the time had come for some Bulgarian wedding music. Leanne and I smiled at each other and decided to stick it out and adapt just as some of the guests from Gill's family had done with American music. At times, as I listened to the music and imitated the dancers around me, I felt as if I were in an Eastern European wedding movie. As in the movies, Caroline and Gill were eventually hoisted up on chairs and carried around as everyone danced and sang. I marveled at the way everyone mixed so well.

Several hours later, at the end of the evening, I danced with Caroline to Donna Summers *Last Dance*. I held Caroline as tightly as I ever had in my life. We did not talk; we just danced. It was an intimate and wonderful experience as we both silently acknowledged the handoff of a daughter from father to husband. The moment that I had most dreaded about my daughter's wedding, the dancing, was now among the most cherished moments of that day. Dancing for me was now an unpredictable experience. The struggle to learn had led to wonderful moments of fun and joy.

When the music and dancing stopped, it started to rain. We boarded the last bus and journeyed up the mountain. We went to bed about three in the morning and woke several hours later to the sounds of Irene. A hurricane in northern Vermont, 200 miles from the ocean, was rare and Irene was her name. We dressed quickly and rushed back to the farmhouse to recoup leftover food, wine, and other possessions. The peaceful river we'd witnessed the day before was now living up to its name, the Mad River. We watched chunks of land break off into the rapids as we moved across the farmland in the swirling wind to reclaim various items. The land on which Caroline and Gill stood for their ceremony was gone, swallowed by the rushing waters. The shallow riverbed downstream, where children played the day before, was a fury of white and brown water rapids. We packed the cars and headed back up the mountain to our hotel, before the road was washed out.

As the day continued, trees would be ripped from the soil and wooden bridges across northern Vermont would collapse. Massive power outages occurred across the northern part of the state and our hotel went dark. Most of our guests were stranded and some didn't get home for five days. We used leftovers to extend the wedding party on Sunday. More than fifty people came to our room throughout the day and ate an assorted mix of appetizers, desserts, and vegetables, and drank champagne served at room temperature by candlelight. The wind and rain made it impossible to go outside.

On Monday afternoon, Eileen and I joined a small caravan of cars and were lucky to find a way over the mountains, avoiding the flooded and mud-filled roads. After a twelve-hour journey, three times the usual trip, we arrived back in Boston late in the evening. On the long slow ride, Eileen and I had plenty of time to talk. For some reason, the words "I might take a few more dance lessons" came out of my mouth. I don't know how but some new voice managed to get past my multi-layered defenses.

Eileen smiled at my thoughts on dance. When Eileen and I first met at a New York City advertising agency, she and her friends would go out dancing nightly. Occasionally I would go with her and watch. I did not dance. At work, her friends called her "Dancin'" because she enjoyed it so much. We quickly fell in love and shared lots of interests, but never dancing. When we announced our engagement, her friends asked her, "How can you marry someone who doesn't dance? Her response was, "Oh, he will. "She was right: she just underestimated how long it would take.

Chapter Four

The Fence-Sitter

Several weeks after the wedding, Eileen mentioned that some of her friends thought that I was continuing to dance just to make her happy. She wanted to know if that was true. I told her I was glad my dancing made her happy, but, in all honesty, I was confused about my feelings about dancing. She found a joy in dancing that I envied, and I didn't know whether I could ever find that joy. While I truly enjoyed dancing at Caroline's wedding, the dance lessons and studio parties beforehand had mostly been a struggle for me, mixed with a sprinkle of fun. I was not convinced that I could learn anything beyond the foxy and knew that, if I tried, it would take serious effort.

Fence-sitters are described as people who take a neutral position or are undecided. That was my mindset about dance. After the wedding, I agreed to take a few more dance lessons from Melissa and attend some dance parties. But I told Melissa, as I'd told Eileen that I did not know if I could find the joy. I knew Melissa would not let me walk out the door without a battle. Dancing had become like an itch that needed to be scratched for me, and she sensed that. The moments of enjoyment and curiosity had been sufficient to keep me engaged for a while. The new voice in my head said maybe I should give it a serious try. A louder, older voice said, *don't do it*. My life was busy, I was happy, and there was no pressure from Eileen to rock the boat. So, why commit to dance lessons and open old wounds at this stage of life?

The older voice was logical. It reminded me that I had no music, dance, or performance experience to draw on. I would need to develop muscle memory and rhythm, learn the new language of dance, and lead a partner. It would mean less time engaging in activities that I enjoyed.

It meant not seeing as much of our friends who were not dancers. There would be periods of immense discomfort, frustration, and embarrassment, with no guarantee of success. And then there was the Dance Dragon who, at any time, could block my path to the dance floor. It made no sense to take up dancing. Why was I hesitating to return to my old life? Eileen offered her view of my situation.

"I'm convinced that another being has taken over your body," she said. "Don't you find your behavior strange? Why are you suddenly interested in pursuing something you avoided for decades? Doesn't it bother you that some men give you funny looks or become quiet when you bring up dancing? What do your squash friends think?"

It was true my behavior had changed; as had my wardrobe. I was wearing solid colored t-shirts under light sweaters to work so I would be comfortably dressed when I went to dance. Some days I wore colored socks that matched the shirts. When I walked around the city, I used earphones to listen to the beat of the music. Squash games were no longer on my calendar but yoga still was. I paid less attention to sporting events. I read about dance history and the meaning of certain dance terms on Wikipedia. I started watching instructional videos on YouTube and dreaming about dance steps.

Eileen was right. My behavior was strange. It was not something that I had planned. It was an unintended consequence of Caroline's wedding. I acknowledged to myself that the entire dance experience was liberating. Yes, I was becoming unpredictable and a bit weird to those that had known me for a long time, but I was also learning about myself.

One night I asked Eileen if she would like to watch a movie called *Born Romantic*. She reminded me that I never watched romantic movies; I had been a lifelong Clint Eastwood fan. I explained that the movie had some funny dance scenes about men trying to learn to dance. Eileen sat up in her chair and told me to put the movie on. The story was set in a salsa club in London where three single men had fallen in love with women who liked to dance. The dance scenes in the movie were funny and the music was great. There is a disco song called *Yes Sir, I Can Boogie* that Eileen and I quickly made our theme song. It was a great pick-me-up tune, and it would energize us to practice. Some nights when we were out with friends, I would take out my iPhone and play the song. Eileen would grab one of her female friends and they would start to boogie the night away. I was too self-conscious as a dancer to participate. I could not figure out how to move my body to the beat. I had an urge, but I had no idea how to satisfy it nor did I understand how that might make me feel.

I found myself trying to initiate conversations on dancing with some male friends outside the studio. They didn't have much insight. Most men I knew did not dance or, on the rare occasion when they did, it was to make a female partner happy. They would mention that they were selective about the music and the dance, as they did not want to make fools out of themselves. A few joked about not wanting to appear unmanly on the dance floor. As for how dancing made these men feel, most could not verbalize an answer. They just gave me a look and moved on.

The more time I spent at the studio, the more I wondered how dancing would make me feel. When I watched experienced dancers move to the music, and interact with each other I wanted to be able to do what they did. I wished to experience how they felt. Before the wedding, I asked dance instructors if I would ever learn to move my body in sync with the rhythm of the music. The answer never seemed as simple as yes or no. "It is possible for you, Dan, but it could be very difficult," Elena told me.

Elena was a spirited young instructor who tried relentlessly to teach me to move in time to the five basic steps of the cha-cha. When we talked, I wondered whether she was really telling me, "Save your time and money. Your dancing is hopeless. " No doubt, Elena would lose her job if she said that outright. There are no hopeless causes in the world of ballroom dancing. Instructors tell you that anyone can learn to dance. It is part of the studio Kool-Aid. Saying otherwise made no business sense.

I was in a beginners' group dance class. Elena was dressed in black, and her pants were too long for her legs. She had dark eyes, black hair, and an "in your face" style that reminded me of women I'd met while living in New York City. I liked her from the moment I saw her. She had been assigned as my alternative instructor to Melissa when I arrived and they were opposites in many ways. She liked to mix up her dance instructions with conversations about life, and she also liked to sing to her students. Elena's family roots could be traced back to Eastern Europe, but she'd grown up in Brooklyn. She talked to her mother every day on the phone. Elena was the shortest person in the entire studio. In class, she moved her feet and, for that matter, all her body parts effortlessly. She was a warm and friendly free spirit.

"Line up behind me and face the mirror," she said to the eight students present. "I want you to walk back and forth across the dance floor. Follow my lead. Now I want you to march left, right, left, right. 1, 2, 3, 4, and 1, 2, 3, 4. I want your left foot to land on the floor on the sound of one and then your right foot on 2. Let's do it again. Wonderful! Wonderful! You are now marching together and your feet are landing on the floor at the same time. There is a rhythm to your marching. Now let us all try marching to music. I will call out the beat. "

She sounded like the drill sergeants I'd had in the army during basic training. Elena played a Latin song, *Es Mentirosa*, a popular meringue song for dancers. The energy picked up in the room. The students smiled at each other and marched to meringue music until the end of the class. Elena told us we had all walked to the beat of the music that night. We discovered we had rhythm, some more than others, but that would change. We didn't know how to walk or march when we were born so we must have learned. Elena told us that next week we would learn to take dance steps to the rhythm of music. Learning to dance is like learning to walk, she said. You do it in a step pattern to a beat. It might be harder for some at first because you need to hear the beat and learn the pattern, but it can be done. I accepted the point of view that I had acquired some rhythm in my lifetime and could learn to overcome at least one barrier in my dance education. How long it would take was another question.

As I was leaving, a fellow student introduced himself. His name was Richie and he was middle-aged. He always wore a baseball cap and had lost his teeth. He was the first man who reached out to help me on the dance floor. In time, his love of dancing would lead Richie to take off his baseball hat on the dance floor and invest in false teeth. Some fall afternoons, I would sit on a bench in the Boston Public Garden and listen to dance music, searching for the beat. Richie would be out walking, and he would come by and sit with me. We would talk about life, our daughters, who had been the reasons we were trying to learn to dance, and our dance experience. In class, I would stand next to him, and he would help me move my feet to the beat. It was important for me to be able to talk openly with other male students about learning to dance. Sometimes I felt the questions in my mind were too stupid to ask in an open class. I appreciated Richie's kindness.

I was in another beginner cha-cha lesson. We would learn the basic steps and then try them with music. Unlike the meringue, where the dancer takes a step on every beat, the basic cha-cha requires you to take five steps to four beats. When I meet new students today and tell them it took me months to learn the basic cha-cha, they think I'm being empathetic; I'm being honest. Elena talked about the *two, three, four and one* where the *four and one* require three steps in the same time as the two steps for the *two, three*. By counting out loud and using the word *and* after the word *four* and before the word *one* we moved our feet three times to two beats and started to train our muscle memory. When I first tried the five steps to her count, my muscles did not respond in a timely fashion. My brain and body were not on the same page. Other students seemed to grasp the concept quickly. I was the odd one out. I thought about my youth and the kids who could not run and dribble a basketball at the same time; now I knew how they felt.

Elena stood in front of the male leaders and demonstrated the steps three times. She then had us follow her, as she watched in the mirror and adjusted her teaching based on what she saw. I caught her looking at me more than the others with her dark eyes. I sensed she had identified me as the outlier. After most of the other students mastered the pattern and the beat, Elena had us practice our steps without partners to the song *Smooth* by Santana. The lyrics "let's don't forget about it" from the song kept ringing in my ear as I tried to remember the steps. I was hopelessly lost but Elena did not call me out. After a few minutes, Elena asked all the male leaders to take a partner. The time had come for me to make a fool of myself. I could smell the foul breath of the Dance Dragon in the room. I saw his shadow on the floor, but no one else noticed. I took a deep breath, let the air out slowly and prepared myself.

In ballroom dance, the male is the leader and must make the first move. His left foot and body weight should be on the floor at the same time as the downbeat, or "one". Elena would count the beat aloud to help those of us who could not hear it. I knew if I did not get off to the right start, it would be difficult to catch up and adjust my body movement to the beat. My partner, if she were willing to play her role of the patient follower, would also have to wait for me, knowing we were off beat. My first partner that night was Jane. She gave me a curious yet sensitive look as if she were asking me in a nice way, "Do you know what you are doing?"

After a few misfires, I finally moved my left foot. I felt as if I was learning to drive a stick-shift car for the first time. It was obvious to Jane that I was still a dance disaster, but she was kind, said nothing for those painful twenty seconds, left me with a thank you, and moved on. I had the opportunity to make a fool of myself with several women I knew and then Eileen was facing me and inquired as to how it was going. Words were not necessary. I just rolled my eyes, groaned, and shook my head sideways. The Dance Dragon was still behind me, hissing, though Eileen did not hear him. The Dance Dragon owned me that evening.

I chose to stay until the end of the class that night and demonstrate my ineptness multiple times to every woman in the room. I considered walking out and leaving the studio. No one would have stopped me. Melissa was not there that night. I might have drawn some attention to myself, but the humiliation would have ended. However, I knew that if I walked out, I would never come back. The Dance Dragon would have a lifelong victory. I reminded myself of the time I made two consecutive errors on groundballs playing third base in Little League. My face burned that day, but I could hear my coach telling me to forget my mistakes. I recovered, and the next day recruited an adult neighbor to hit groundballs for me to field. Practice, practice, practice, I told myself.

At the end of class, Richie sensed my frustration and offered to stay behind and practice with me. We marched for a while and then tried a few cha-cha steps. I truly appreciated his effort, but I was emotionally spent that evening. I left the studio with Eileen, confused about the beat, the footwork, and my own inability to process the basics like the other students. I gave myself an F in the class that night. The only bright spot that dark evening was how helpful everyone in that room had been to me.

Frustration lingered on for several days. It was one thing to make a fool of myself in a private lesson with Melissa, which, remarkably, I had gotten used to. It was totally different to embarrass myself with multiple women in a single lesson. The sources of my frustration were my timing and a lack of consistency with step sequence. Eventually, I would learn to listen to the count of the instructor in my lessons and remember many of the steps, but in social situations I would be on my own. I would be the leader who could not lead his dance partner. The class with Elena had reminded me of my worst dance nightmares. The dragon was back in my head and he was bigger than ever. I had hardly noticed him since Caroline's wedding.

I needed to stop fence-sitting. Ambivalence was driving me crazy. One night, I had fun and sensed progress. The next night I'd be totally frustrated. The sources of my own discontent varied. It could be my inability to remember steps. It could be the feeling of awkwardness with a certain dance partner. If I was going to continue to inflict pain or discomfort on myself, I needed to have a purpose going forward. Caroline's wedding was history. At the next party, I found myself dancing with Laura Colcord, a top-level dancer and someone who had been dancing for a decade. I asked Laura why she thought so many more women than men danced.

Laura told me that in her experience men gave up too quickly. They didn't hang in there long enough to overcome their feelings of awkwardness and learn to enjoy dancing. She reminded me that dance was an acquired experience, and that, before I judged it, I must give it serious effort.

When I was young, I listened to my male friends talk about feeling awkward and self-conscious on the dance floor. My male peers understood the feeling, disliked it, and empathized with each other, so we gave each other permission to opt out. Dancing, unlike smoking cigarettes or drinking a six-pack of beer, was not one of the rituals we associated with achieving manhood. Unlike sports, it was okay to just quit dancing. Intentionally or not, Laura had thrown me a challenge.

The idea that dancing was an acquired experience made me think. I took up skiing when I was 37. It required a lot of effort. Occasionally, I made a fool out of myself getting off a lift chair and fell in front of a crowd. A few times, I got frostbite, which was physically painful. Sometimes, when I tried to ski through the moguls on a steep slope, I lost control, fell and slid down the mountain. In time, I found my balance and rhythm, and connected to the snow, ice, and wind around me. I acquired a love for skiing, but it took a few seasons. A voice, the new one inside me, wondered, *could dance be like that?*

The next morning as I drank my coffee, I started to thumb through a book, *Ballroom Dancing: The Romance, Rhythm, And Style* by John Lawrence Reynolds. Joey Nowlin, one of the male instructors at the studio, had passed it on to me. Joey was an enthusiastic and creative instructor who had found his way from Arkansas to Massachusetts. He was always trying to find ways to motivate students to make dance a part of their lives. The book covered the history of ballroom dancing and featured some great photographs of dance costumes and various dance positions. Those aspects of the book did not interest me. However, I found a quote in the book that captured my attention about both dance and life.

"If we stand on the sidelines and simply wish, nothing will change. If we choose to participate without training and practice, growing merely frustrated, nothing will be learned. But if we move past the twin barriers of intimidation and frustration, we may discover new vistas, new pleasures and new aspects of ourselves and others. "

Reynolds was right. Without a commitment to train and practice, I could not expect to learn and frustration would prevail. If I wanted to get past the Dance Dragon and discover the joy of dance, I needed to trust that, with time and effort, I could make it happen. I needed to get off the fence about dancing. Two days later, when I saw Melissa, I told her I wanted to commit to a program that would result in my becoming a good social dancer. I wanted to make dance a part of my life.

Chapter Five

Back to the Beginning

I walked across the floor with unsettled eyes, raised my left arm slowly and offered my hand. We danced the waltz and I glanced at Melissa while she processed every move I made. I felt like the Tin Man in *The Wizard of Oz*. I could walk, but I was stiff. It was excruciatingly painful being watched, but that was how we began. I wondered whether Melissa could turn me into a dancer? Melissa believed in herself, her mentors, and the studio curriculum. That was a great foundation for her. However, she was light on experience and I could offer nothing other than my best effort.

We had agreed to start fresh with the waltz. I needed to learn to be a dancer in contrast to just walking steps in a pre-determined pattern. Dance was about moving my entire body, not just my feet. Melissa mentioned that in time we would do a solo waltz performance at the studio. She had big dreams for me. I did not share those dreams. I never saw myself performing on any dance stage. The idea of a solo performance sometime in the future was terrifying. I didn't reject Melissa's suggestion of a performance on the spot, and that was a big mistake. No comment meant "yes" to a dance instructor. Melissa, like all the instructors at the studio, was trained to practice the art of assumptive sales.

The idea of moving my body in time to music in front of a large audience of my peers intimidated me. It was counter to everything I had done in my life. I would never volunteer to do it. Why would Melissa think I would want to embarrass myself in such a way? I knew embarrassment well, but it had always been accidental, not intentional. My mild-mannered instructor was unpredictably frightening at times. I wondered how much of her personality on the job was her own and how much had been shaped by the studio.

The day before my waltz lesson, I tried to imagine myself as Richard Gere doing the waltz in the movie *Shall We Dance*. My imagination failed me. Gere's struggle to learn to dance in the movie was inspirational, but I could not envision myself doing a waltz or, for that matter, being Richard Gere. I gave up on Gere and decided to listen to the song *Come Away with Me* by Norah Jones several times to get in the mood for my waltz lesson. I tried to identify the 1, 2, 3 beat in the music, with mixed results.

Lessons at the studio usually started with a warm-up dance. Melissa would try to figure me out from the moment I arrived. That night was no exception. As we danced in a box to the rumba, Melissa asked me about my day and then complimented me on my salmon-colored t-shirt. As usual, she kept the conversation fixated on me as she played the role of my social dance partner. As a male beginner who was thinking about too many dance things at the same time, intelligent conversation on my part was not possible. Melissa then switched her role from dance partner to instructor and asked me to walk across the floor and invite her to dance the waltz. I saw the familiar look of patience and support. There was never a hint of anger, boredom, or frustration on her face, regardless of how often I messed up. That evening, after we danced for a few minutes, Melissa stopped and provided some suggestions.

"After you put out your left hand, you want to stand tall and still and wait for your partner to approach. Your arms should be extended with your elbows almost parallel to your shoulders but not so far back that you couldn't see them out of the corners of your eyes. Keep your head and shoulders back and your shoulders down. Let your partner chose how close to stand, and then place your right hand with fingers closed on her shoulder blade. Let's try and focus on a few of these things, one thing at a time".

I repeated my approach several times, remembering some of the points Melissa suggested. I also focused on the location and movement of my left arm. I sensed Melissa knew my mind was not 100 percent focused on what she had asked me to do, but initially she said nothing. I had become aware of my tentative left arm movement a few nights before in a group class. A female student had tried to help by suggesting I use both my arms to provide a solid dance frame, and those comments were still in my head.

When the approach drill ended, I asked Melissa about my left arm position. Her reply was that we could deal with it later, and I needed to stay focused on correcting what she had suggested. We would run through the same drill again. Melissa did not talk like a drill sergeant, but she had her way of being firm.

Looking back, the need for me to concentrate on the subject taught in a specific lesson was a constant theme with Melissa and other instructors. My usual scatter-brained approach to learning by absorbing everything around me in a random fashion was not going to work. At the studio, dancers often offered me real-time advice. I would then immediately stop practicing whatever I was doing and tried to incorporate their suggestions in my dance. The more advice I received, the more cluttered my brain became. Initially, I was obsessed with learning everything and confident that, in time, I could connect all the information. The problem was that the advice came from both qualified and unqualified sources. It was also the result of disconnected dance experiences at parties and group dances and not necessarily related to any lesson plan. I needed to focus on what was being taught in real time and save my questions about other dance moves for later.

Later in that lesson, Melissa circled back and asked me about my left arm. I explained I was a left-handed person, and I usually lead with that arm and hand to do most routine activities. In dance, I was unsure as to how best to lead with my left arm and how much pressure or strength I should place behind it to direct my partner. I did not want to push and pull my partner, nor did I want my arm and hand to be wimpy. I needed to find the right balance. I mentioned my recent experience in a group class with Piera, an outgoing and attractive woman from Italy who worked at the Italian consulate in Boston.

Piera had noticed my weak frame in a group class and suggested that my "floppy" left arm, as she called it, was the source of my problem. Piera liked to dance close to men and preferred male dance partners with strong dance frames. With that in mind, Piera, speaking in a combination of Italian and English, instructed me on how to use my arms to improve my frame. We practiced moving my left arm into different positions and then, with both arms up and locked in what I referred to as the touchdown position, we danced. By the end of the class, Piera was happy with my progress and let me know she was willing to "invest" herself in my dance development. Piera told me more than once that dancing with any man was preferable to no man. I smiled politely back at her. Melissa knew Piera and found my story amusing. With a few refinements and suggestions, Melissa confirmed that Piera had sent me in the right direction.

We returned to the lesson plan, and Melissa requested that I lead her through an underarm turn and this time watch myself in the mirror. As I led her through the turn with my eyes on the mirror, I noticed that my shoulders had risen and were almost touching my ears, my head was tilted forward toward the floor and my butt stuck out. My body posture reminded me of the banana-like dance posture of my youth. Melissa, with her straight-back posture, looked six inches taller than I. The horrifying picture of myself in the mirror remained fixed in my mind. All I could do was grunt, close my eyes, and shake my head.

I was motivated to fix the problem immediately. I asked Melissa if we could do the underarm turn one more time. I repeated my "one more time" request six more times. On the seventh repeat, as I looked in the mirror I saw that my head was up, my arms locked in a touchdown frame, and my shoulders were back. I still felt stiff but the banana look was gone. I had erased the awful memory in my mind temporarily.

That night I left the dance floor with a body that was both tense and exhausted and a brain that had gone off the track. For 45 minutes, the wires in my brain had received a massive amount of information and delivered much of it to my body. I needed to regroup, reduce the turmoil in my head, and focus on training certain body parts and strengthening others. At the end of the lesson, I glanced at Melissa's face several times. I saw patience. Words were not necessary.

At my next lesson, I was determined to focus the warm-up dance conversation on Melissa rather than myself. I succeeded in getting Melissa to talk about herself briefly. I learned that mint chocolate chip was her favorite ice cream. Melissa then assumed her role as my instructor, looked me in the eyes and outlined the lesson plan for the day. We would work on relaxing my tense body, muscle development to support better posture, and leading my partner in dance with my core.

Somehow Melissa seemed to hypnotize me during the lesson. For the next few weeks, whenever I heard the word "relax" in my dreams, at work, or saying it to myself at class, I found myself rolling my head back and forth and sideways. Sometimes I also moved my shoulders up, back, and down repeatedly until there was no tension in my shoulders or back. I moved my arms in toward my chest and then out while I kept my elbows in place and breathed. I also tried to train myself to turn my mind off, relax, stop anticipating, and trust my body with the music.

In my previous lesson, I had witnessed my banana-like posture in the mirror. The picture was permanently implanted in my mind. Melissa now knew all she had to do was mention that image, and she had my attention. Dancers need to maintain their posture for the entire dance. That requires strong back muscles to maintain a straight back and keep one's head up and over their shoulders. My lifelong indifference to body bearing, and, more recently, long hours spent on the computer and phone, had taken their toll on my posture. Whenever I looked at Melissa, I saw a person with a straight back, head up and centered. She became my role model.

Melissa asked me to place my hands on her upper back and introduced me to her lats, the muscle that forms a triangle from the shoulders down to the hips. Properly developed and strengthened, our lats can help hold up our shoulders and keep our backs straight. Melissa placed her fingers on my lat muscles and let me draw my own conclusions. Despite a lifetime of daily exercise, my upper back muscles were weak. I was not prepared to move across the floor in a waltz, hold my arms up and out, and breathe while keeping my back straight for most of a three-minute dance.

I asked how long it might take me to strengthen my muscles. Melissa told me that she didn't always have her current posture and had worked hard on back-muscle development and posture while commuting on the subway. I tried to picture Melissa on the MBTA Blue Line working on her posture. I smiled to myself, impressed with her inner drive. Little did I know that within a few months I would also find myself practicing posture and dance steps on the MBTA platform as I waited for the train.

I would be indifferent to the people around me. Dance would turn me into a subway weirdo.

Next, we talked about the ten-pound weight of a human head and how the trapezoid muscles that run between the neck and shoulders help a person hold that head up. I thought about all the men walking on the street that I pass everyday with their heads hanging down and wondered about their trapezoid muscles. I then looked at the way Melissa held her head up. My choice was clear; I would follow her advice.

For most of my life strengthening the core of my body was not part of any conversation. I never took a course in biology or human anatomy in school. In sports, I did not recollect anyone using the term. It was not until I took up yoga that core strength became a focus, and even then, I did not connect it to a specific athletic need. Before dance, I was mostly ignorant about the role my core played in my life.

My arms were a different story. I played baseball, tennis, squash, and golf at different times in my life and developed the strength to swing a bat, racquet or club effectively. Everyday activity had instilled in me a tendency to move and lift everything with my arms. On the dance floor, I initially used my arms to direct, pull or push my partner rather than shift weight with my core and knees to communicate direction and pace. In dance, Melissa explained, I must learn to lead my partner with my core, which was concentrated in my belly and lower and middle back.

Melissa placed her hands on my shoulders and asked me to drop my arms by my side and dance. It was a weird new sensation. My core and legs moved to the music, and my shifting weight would signal Melissa to move directionally at a certain pace. Conceptually, I understood what Melissa was telling me. I had to lead with my core and legs and use my arms to maintain a tight upper frame for partners like Piera to dance within. If I wanted to be a dancer, my body needed to learn new ways of doing things and drop old habits.

When I left the studio that afternoon, I had a better understanding of the role my mind and body played in dance. I saw that dancing began before the music did. It started with managing my mindset, relaxing and driving the tension away, with how I carried my body on to the floor, and how I prepared to physically connect with my partner. Dancing was not just about music, muscle memory, and rhythm. It was also about posture, head position, a straight back, and a solid frame.

As I walked home, I passed some young girls on the way to the Boston Ballet studio. I observed their posture, the way they walked, and how they kept their heads back on their shoulders. I was jealous. They stood out on the street, walking among the many adults with forward-leaning heads and slouched shoulders. I had a flashback to my time in the military, the way people walked and the energy in their gait. I had forgotten the importance of posture and resolved that I must work on it. I would stand straight from the top of my head down through my shoulders, hips, and knees. In the future when I asked a potential female dance partner to dance, I wanted them to look at my posture, read my body language, say yes, and jump out of their chair. I wanted to shock the Dance Dragon the next time I walked on the dance floor.

Chapter Six

The Tribe

A thin layer of dance confidence had formed within me. At a studio dance party, I approached Eileen and asked if she would like to do the tango. It was a bold move for me, but it was met with enthusiastic support. Eileen was both my strongest supporter, and on occasion my biggest critic, albeit a constructive one. She was often frustrated with my slow pace of learning dance. She knew me as a quick learner and an athlete. I knew doing a tango dance with her would elicit either a strong positive or a strong negative response. At first, she had met my interest in dance with skepticism and adopted a wait-and-see attitude. Initially she joined me at the studio for group classes and parties, and in time came to realize I was committed to learn. Eileen decided to pursue her own dance experience through private lessons and performances. She loved dancing the tango, as taught to her by Fran, her instructor.

Melissa had convinced me that I was ready for Thursday night parties and dancing with the more experienced dancers. I uttered the mantra of the dance studio to myself: *"relax, have fun, and enjoy yourself.* "After all, that was the promise of ballroom dancing. I listened to the music, visualized myself as a great dancer, and then moved my left heel forward as I led Eileen into the tango with my new improved posture. The tango is a dance of passion, strength, and confidence. I had recently watched Antonio Banderas dance the tango in the movie *Take the Lead* and Al Pacino in *Scent of a Woman*. I wasn't qualified to judge their technical dance expertise, but they captured the style and passion that I fantasized I would portray in a tango dance one day.

My interest in the tango received a boost after reading *Twelve Minutes of Love* by Kapka Kassabova. The book had been a gift from

Caroline for Fathers' Day. It is a story of a young woman born in Bulgaria who migrates to New Zealand and becomes addicted to the tango. Her desire for a perfect tango experience takes her to three continents where she experiences moments of dance joy, frustration, and love. Along the way, Kapka receives an education about life that keeps the reader turning the pages. Many of the people Kapka meets have "tango mania"; such people are called "tangolistas. "While the causes for the addiction vary, they often center on a person's fantasies, yearnings and feelings for another person. The tango allows a person to experience their fantasy and feel passion and love. The better the dance, the more intense the feeling.

The tango had become a serious "must do" in the lives of the tangolistas. Kassabova's mental, physical, and emotional efforts to learn and feel the experience of the tango provided a view for me of a different way of life. As I turned the pages, I began to understand how a dance could become so important to a person's reason to live, and how these tangolistas could find so much joy in dance. I had no illusions about becoming a great tango dancer, but I wanted to accompany this young writer on her journey so I could better understand the power dance held over certain people. Kapka and the tangolistas reminded me of Jack Kerouac and his quote in *On the Road* that hung on my office wall for many years.

> "*The only people for me are the mad ones, the ones who are mad to live, mad to talk, mad to be saved. The ones who never yawn or say a commonplace thing, but burn like fabulous Roman candles.* "

Kapka Kassabova's portraits of tango characters in her book reminded me of Kerouac's "mad ones". Kerouac saw that living without the burn of intense feelings and passion was not a life. The tangolistas did not pursue the ordinary nor did they yawn. They gave up everything, not just to dream. but to pursue their dream. They accepted the struggle as much as the reward. Kapka Kassabova, in Kerouac's terms, was a "mad one. "A part of me wanted to experience that burn, that madness with dance, or at least to understand it, even if only for twenty or thirty seconds.

My mind returned to my own tango. I focused on the music and intended to turn my mind off and let my body take over once I got going. I kept repeating "slow, slow, quick, quick, slow" to the beat. I told myself to bend my knees, look away from my partner in a cool and aloof way, and project male confidence and attitude by locking in my frame. Unfortunately, I overloaded my brain and forgot about my traveling direction as I moved on the floor. I unconsciously started to dance clockwise when all the other couples were dancing counterclockwise. I was dancing into the middle of oncoming floor traffic.

Eileen rolled her eyes and told me in a critical voice that I was dancing against the line of dance and needed to dance in the same direction as everyone else. Like most men, my reaction to a female comment on directions did not sit well. I mistakenly thought I could go in whatever direction I chose. Plus, I was trying to project male confidence. I was dancing the tango like Antonio Banderas. Eileen was more concerned with the details of specific direction and steps. Her comments were a distraction from my achieving my dream. I was the leader on the dance floor, and her role was to follow. I needed to create the perception that I knew what I was doing, even if I was wrong. After about thirty seconds of mental struggle, Melissa tapped me on the shoulder and suggested that I reverse directions and follow the line of dance. I grunted and nodded.

Dancing the tango was hard. There were fantasy roles to play, steps to take on time, a posture to maintain, and of course the need to avoid other couples on the floor. I needed to get past all the mental and physical aspects of dance if I wanted to experience the emotional power of the tango.

I thought about my experience on the dance floor that night as I walked home. There were some good dancers on the floor. I was clearly not one of them. While I did not experience any of the "fun and relaxing" aspect of dance, and there were moments ranging from awkwardness to acute embarrassment, I had dealt with it. I had tried to approach the dance floor with confidence and screwed up. Fortunately, I was dancing with Eileen and she told me what I had to hear even if I did not want to hear it. My journey to become a competent social dancer would have tense moments. As for the feeling that the tangolistas found in the tango, that was a distant but worthy goal. I wanted to acquire that feeling, and I was just beginning to understand the effort it would take to make that happen. What was unusual to me was the fact that none of the good dancers seemed to disapprove, or told me to "get my act together. "They had encouraged me to keep trying. This was a different type of crowd. I asked myself, *"Who were these people? What made them tick?"*

I had trouble sleeping after Thursday night dance parties. I can't explain it. Sometimes I thought it was a body chemical thing, like running, when my body took in a lot of oxygen, and I got a natural high. Sometimes I thought it was emotional because I had so many ups and downs on the dance floor. I usually lay in bed and daydreamed about dance until peace came. That Thursday night, I thought about dance studio cultures and tribes. I had visited other studios around Boston to attend their weekend dance parties and their cultures were similar. As a marketing professional, one of the first things I did was to try and segment and prioritize the audiences within a crowd. In dance studios, I had identified the "wedding people. " They were learning to perform a single dance or two because dance was required or expected from them at a specific event. I was once a wedding person. Wedding people as a segment don't have a lot of impact on dance culture because they are short-timers. However, they do make studios a lot of money.

After Caroline's wedding, I chose to go back to the studio, but I was unclear as to why. I became what I called a "fence-sitter. " Most instructors work hard at trying to provide fence-sitters with sufficient reasons to make dance a part of life, but the ambivalence of a fence-sitter makes the path to dance happiness unclear. As a group, they have little impact on a dance-studio culture because of their ambivalence. I had been a fence-sitter for a time, but that phase had passed.

The dancers in the studio tribe I had become most interested in were the "committed ones. " I saw these dancers as a bit off-center, because the people in mainstream America who don't dance often considered those who dance frequently to be a bit eccentric. "Committed ones" are eccentric because, all things considered, these dancers would rather dance in their free time than do most other things. The committed ones seldom go to movies, watch television, or hang out with people from work after hours at the bar because they are dancing, practicing, or taking lessons. At the studio, cultural background or profession was not relevant. Dance students came from Vermont, Alabama and California, as well as Turkey, China and Canada. They were doctors, university students, cake makers, and construction workers. They had strayed from the mainstream herd and entered the world of ballroom dancing. Perhaps they were at a transition point in life or searching for something different and discovered ballroom dancing. They publicly acknowledged their passion, or what you might call their addiction, to dance. I wanted to better understand the passion of the "committed ones" and what they derived from dancing. I could only do that if I traveled among them.

In most studios, there is a small hardcore group of dancers. Perhaps there were ten to twelve in my studio. I labeled them the "mad ones" like the characters in Kerouac's book. The group could probably not survive in a studio on their own. They lacked a critical mass, and there was a shortage of male partners. Some of them went to multiple studios for different reasons. It also takes considerable time, money, and self-discipline to be a "mad one." Most of them burn with passion for dance for a period and then revert to being among the "committed ones." They are like Kassabova's tangolistas in that they are seriously addicted to experiencing the feel of the dance and they have the resources to pursue their passion. Mary, the software engineer, was a short lady with red hair and a big laugh, and was a highly competitive performer. Jonas, the tall one, who spoke Lithuanian, built a practice dance floor in his garage. Jeff, the former Wall Street executive turned personal trainer; Laura, a Fulbright scholar who started dancing after she reached forty, and now competes whenever she can. Cliff, the urologist, and Jen, the hand surgeon, were among the "mad ones" in the studio. And of course, there was Lola. Initially I thought she was a "committed one" but in time I would realize that she too wanted to feel the burn and was truly a "mad one. " I wondered how long the "mad ones" could live without dancing. Their passion for dance was perpetual.

Along with the instructors, I saw the core tribe in most studios consisting of "committed ones" and "mad ones", both sharing the responsibility for evolving the studio tribe culture. The goals were to grow the tribe, support each other's dance development and help the "mad ones" get through a night or weekend of dance when there was a shortage of partners.

I woke up Friday morning about five and put the coffee on. The rumba was the subject of my afternoon lesson that day, and I needed to practice. Otherwise, whatever I learned in my last lesson would be a blur and we would waste time backtracking. I had decided weeks ago that the only time for me to practice dance was early in the morning before I left for work. I moved the furniture into a corner, read my notes, and waited for the sun to rise and fill the room with light. I returned to the bedroom around 6:30 and asked Eileen if she would like to practice with me. Her reactions to my morning requests were unpredictable. She liked to sleep. That morning she was tough and told me that no one in his or her right mind would wake someone up this early and expect him or her to dance. I acknowledged that I was being a bit selfish but I had no choice. I could not be found dancing by myself in the office. Plus, she knew the steps far better than I did and could correct me. Sometimes compliments work with Eileen.

I played Lionel Richie's song *You Are* and started to rumba. I pressed my feet down into the floor as I bent one knee and then the other. We did a few basic moves and then a cross-body lead. Eileen would tell me if I was on beat and provide feedback on the timing of my weight shifts, and I would try to correct myself. We practiced for twenty to thirty minutes. Eileen's feedback that morning consisted of a random mix of positive and negative comments. Eileen was usually less patient in the morning. After my morning practice, I walked to work, occasionally stopping to dance a few steps.

Later that day, I arrived at the studio for my lesson. During our warm-up dance, Melissa asked me how I liked the dance party the previous night. I told her that dancing against the line of dance had been momentarily embarrassing, but I'd liked the people. They were very supportive. I had danced with more than twenty women, and that was hard for me given the fact that many of them were the better dancers. In the studio, I was also beginning to separate the regulars from the short-timers, and was learning to approach different dance partners with different expectations.

Melissa nodded at my comments and then switched gears and became the instructor. I looked in the mirror to check that there was no evidence of a banana-like posture, and we worked on the rumba. I was glad I had practiced in the morning. I moved my feet reasonably well and kept to the beat.

That night I mentioned to Eileen that I thought many of the people at the party were committed to learning and having fun. There were also fewer people with big egos than I expected. I suggested we spend more time dancing and socializing with other students, to reduce my need to wake her up in the mornings to practice. Eileen agreed.

My thoughts on dance tribes and studio culture had been impacted by yet another dance novel I had recently read. *Mambo Peligroso* was written by Patricia Chao and given to me by my son Tim and his wife Erin. Tim is a journalist and we lived in New York where the story is set when he was a child. The story is about a fictitious character named Catalina Midori who, like the author, is of Japanese-Cuban decent. Her Japanese mother had shaped Catalina's youth, and she had lost touch with her Cuban roots.

Catalina was living an ordinary life on the Upper West Side of Manhattan in 1997 when she discovered her passion for the mambo at the famous Copacabana club on 57th Street. Catalina knew no one in the mambo world, but within a few months she'd joined a local mambo dance tribe and become addicted. I saw Midori as one of Kerouac's "mad ones", just like Kassabova's tangolistas. She reminded me of the "mad ones" at the studio. After reading the book I asked Eileen if she found it more than coincidental that both my children would pick out books for me for Father's Day that focused on an individual who joined a dance tribe, became addicted, and changed their lives. Her response was a smile and a nod.

We talked more about joining the studio dance tribe. There was a social component to both learning and experiencing dance that we had underestimated. For us, the social aspect of a diverse urban dance studio crowd would become as important as taking lessons. Eileen and I were not tribe people. We avoided exclusive groups and disliked any environment where conformity was the price of social acceptance. Eileen had grown up in New York City and was blessed with city smarts, a quick sense of humor, and a tendency to speak her mind. She liked people who were direct and open, and who could laugh at themselves. The studio had its share of such people. It didn't require that we be great dancers or have a certain income. I sensed Eileen was closer to becoming addicted to dance than she publicly acknowledged, but both of us had to commit or neither would. For Eileen and me, the commitment to support tribe members and instructors was not something we could fake. It meant allocating time to learning, attending studio events where solos were performed, and helping both members of the tribe and new dancers.

Eileen reminded me of her friend's husband who had decided he wanted to learn to dance. He took weekly lessons with his instructor for six months. He never socialized or danced with other ballroom people. He would invite his instructor to a business event or a neighborhood or family party and he would only dance with her, no one else. Eileen's friend was dumbfounded, and her husband could not explain why he avoided dancing with any other women. Eventually the wife convinced him that his dependency on his instructor was not a good thing. If he wanted to be a social dancer, then he had to learn to dance with others. Being a smart husband, he listened to his wife. He abandoned dancing, and doubled his time on the golf course.

We realized the option existed just to continue to take private lessons with our instructors and dance socially with each other occasionally. There were perhaps half-a-dozen serious dancers at the studio who danced only with an instructor or their spouse. Eileen's story about her friend's husband contained several messages. It was highly unlikely that I could learn to be a good social dancer if I limited my dance experience to Melissa and Eileen. Each dance partner was unique, and the more partners I danced with, the more I learned. A side benefit of such an approach would be that it would allow Eileen to sleep later.

My second major takeaway was that while Eileen's friend's husband took dance lessons, he missed much of the joy of ballroom dance by not joining a tribe. I can understand why he returned to golf, as dancing only with an instructor does not allow you to truly connect with the dance world. Perhaps if he had read about the tangolistas or Catalina, the mambo dancer, or danced at a Thursday evening party, he would have found more joy in dancing.

Eileen's parable made the decision easy. We would commit to joining the tribe and do our best to support and learn from other dancers. How could I defeat the Dance Dragon if I did not dance with other people? How could I experience the passion and joy of dancing if I limited whom I danced with? Kapka Kassabova, Catalina Midori, and all the "committed ones" and "mad ones" at the studio came to understand the joy of dancing by challenging themselves, being open-minded, and dancing with different people. They joined dance tribes. Ultimately Eileen and I would need to do the same thing. What I did not know at the time was just how many women I would dance with.

Chapter Seven

Praise Sandwiches

The men in the room were an odd lot in terms of age, dress, musical knowledge and skill at dance. It took me a few months to figure them out. As members of the tribe, they shared a desire to learn dance, become good leaders on the dance floor, and support each other. In the shoe room, the restroom, and at the water cooler these men talked about the challenge of leading a female partner, particularly when she was the better dancer. They talked about instructors, their personalities and how every instructor buried them in praise, regardless of their skill or effort. For reality checks, they tended to rely on each other, a few trusted female partners and a girlfriend or spouse.

One day, I decided to reach out to Jonas, a respected member of the tribe, and ask for his perspective on tribal culture, praise, and its impact on men. Jonas Biekus was a "mad one. "As a child, Jonas's parents took him to as many Lithuanian folk dance events as possible. In college, Jonas would dance the hustle at night and study John Travolta's moves in *Saturday Night Fever* during the day. On occasion, Jonas arrived at a studio party in his white suit ready to dance the hustle. At six feet five inches, he was the tallest dancer at the studio and among the most gracious on the floor. Women at the studio described Jonas as having a dry sense of humor, though he initially came across as shy. They loved to dance with him because he was polite, knew what he was doing and was always willing to help others learn.

"You will never see people here criticize another dancer. All the students in the studio are praised regardless of their ability or their progress. In exchange, the culture requires that everyone must dance at the studio even if they suck at it. That is not easy. Dancers need support, and simply by showing up they earn it. For beginners, the support keeps them coming back until they reach some level of confidence and the urge to dance grows within them. For more experienced dancers, some objective criticism needs to be delivered but it always comes within a sandwich of praise. "

Jonas's use of the term "a sandwich of praise" was both accurate and memorable. I appreciated the need for any instructor to build confidence with any student, whether it was in the classroom, in sports, or at a dance studio. Yet, when it came to dance, I often wondered if a steady diet of praise might be an overdose. Men know how they feel on the dance floor. If that feeling does not improve, praise was a poor substitute. Over time, a few other men helped shape my development as a leader.

Next to Jonas, Ramsey was probably the tallest man in the room. He was younger than me and could have been a descendant of the pharaohs. Ramsey was raised in Tripoli. His father was from North Africa, and his mother was born in Colombia. When he found himself in South America with his Colombian cousins, they tried to teach him to dance, but there was never enough time. Ramsey moved to Montreal for college and wanted to learn to dance but the opportunities were limited. When he later moved to Boston, he decided he had run out of excuses. He had to learn.

Mathias was close to Ramsey in age. French by birth, he had spent his early years in Africa living in multiple countries where his mother worked for Club Med. His parents died suddenly and Mathias went to live with his grandfather in Hong Kong. He attended boarding school in Switzerland before coming to the U. S. for college. His interest in dance came from listening to his grandfather talk about the importance of dance in his life as a young French soldier.

Mike was born in Indiana, grew up in Pennsylvania, attended Syracuse University in New York, and was among the few married men at the studio. After college, he found himself in Danbury, Connecticut, where he met Natalie. Mike originally avoided dance but, like other men in the tribe, a woman had motivated him to try to learn ballroom. Natalie, a young fun-loving Cuban-American woman, was raised in New Jersey and enjoyed clubbing and disco dancing in Manhattan with her Latin friends. On the nights Natalie was out clubbing, Mike was back in Danbury, Connecticut, secretly taking beginner ballroom dance lessons. Years after they married, they agreed to take dance lessons together at the studio.

Unlike most men in the tribe, Cliff had embraced ballroom as a youth. He grew up in San Diego and later attended Stanford University. He loved music and played in the Stanford band. At the time, there was not much opportunity to do ballroom dancing in Palo Alto, so Cliff went to San Francisco on weekends whenever he could. After college, he pursued a career as a doctor, and his journey took him to the East Coast. Life was busy in Boston with his profession and then marriage and a child, so his passion for dance was deferred. Years later, he walked into the studio, put on his dance shoes, and seldom missed a dance lesson. Cliff quickly became one of the "mad ones" in the tribe. He was a good leader on the dance floor but wanted to be among the best.

The role of leaders and followers in ballroom dance has not changed over the years. When there are not enough male leaders in the room, experienced female dancers fill the role. Leaders line up on one side of the room and the followers or females on the opposite side. Men never play the role of followers. Instructors teach the leaders and followers their respective steps and body moves, and then bring them together to practice as couples. Whenever there was down-time between lessons, I chatted with the other leaders, shared dance experiences, and on occasion talked about the confusing language of dance. Sometimes men would demonstrate steps or body moves to each other to validate that both the language and the activity were correct. I soon realized that I was not alone in my fear of dance and my struggle to learn. I suspected that a few leaders, men who felt awkward on the dance floor, may have had dragons in their heads as well. I enjoyed the male company and found humor in our collective mishaps. My motivation to learn and improve grew with the efforts of the men around me.

Ramsey and Mathias were comparable dancers and, like me, Melissa was their instructor. Both men saw social dancing as a skill worth developing and wanted to be prepared to share the dance experience with female companions. They were single, athletic, and self–confident, except when it came to dance. Mathias, a former competitive kick boxer who'd suffered one broken jaw too many, had great balance and could easily shift his weight in a timely fashion. However, he felt awkward on the dance floor. Mathias did not hide the fact that he found learning ballroom dancing to be scarier than kickboxing. As he once explained "physical pain hurts, but making a fool of yourself in front of others is a different type of pain." Mathias's thoughts on making a fool of himself resonated with me, as well as with most other men in the class. I asked Mathias what he had learned from kickboxing that he found relevant to dance.

"Both dance and kickboxing require that you physically connect with your opponent in the ring or with your partner on the dance floor. However, unlike kickboxing where you connect with strength and force, dance requires that you connect with the slightest amount of pressure and grace so that only your partner knows you, as the leader, want to shift direction or adjust the speed of movement. I want to learn to dance well enough to connect with my partner so that she will have confidence in my ability to lead her on the dance floor. "

Ramsey also had an athletic background. Soccer was his passion. I assumed he was an unselfish player because that is the way he was in the dance world. Ramsey always kept his cool, danced with everyone and avoided any collisions. If there were an award for studio gentleman of the year, Ramsey would be a top contender. After most group classes, Ramsey would ask the instructor to repeat the moves and steps they had taught, along with their commentary. He would video them, and then distribute his videos to those of us in the class who valued them.

Ramsey would share his dance frustrations with me. We discovered we both possessed a common shortcoming in dance: we could not always hear the beat and that made learning to dance more difficult. Andru and Joy, instructors at the studio, had gone out of their way to explain beat and music tempo to me. Conceptually, I understood, but I needed more work. I needed to experiment. I empathized with Ramsey on hearing the beat and let him know what I had done.

Eileen had been aware of my frustration with the difficulty of understanding beat and timing. She mentioned one day that Bob Grady, a colleague of hers, might be a resource. Bob was an artist by day and a serious Argentine tango dancer at night. Bob's wife was not a tango dancer so his tango dance partner was a young musician in Boston named Laura Bouix. Laura was an accomplished music teacher and educator with degrees in both from McGill University in Canada. She was a band director with the Boston public schools and spent summers as a director of a youth orchestra in Vermont. Eileen suggested we reach out to Bob and Laura and see if they could help.

Several weeks later, I found myself listening to Laura play the flute at Bob Grady's studio in Boston. Laura would ask me to march, often to tango music, and Bob would walk behind me with his hands on my shoulders adjusting my pace to the music. It was a bit weird at first, but I was desperate. Sometimes I would listen to the music and lead and other times I would try and match Bob's body movement. It was a trial and error approach. Collectively we made progress. Laura had strong beliefs about the need to teach every child music and how different children came to class with different knowledge levels of music. Her challenge, which she accepted enthusiastically, was to help each child find its own way to appreciate music for life. She believed adults could also learn, regardless of their background, though she acknowledged it may take longer. We had four or five sessions together and the four of us laughed a lot in the process. Laura and Bob instilled in me a belief that I could learn the basic patterns of music. I told Ramsey I was going to keep working on the beat and invited him to join me.

Cliff, a surgeon and accomplished amateur musician, joined the tribe about the same time I did. He was determined to make up for lost time in his dance life but confessed that he was intimidated by the quality of the dancers he saw when he first walked through the door. I smiled when he told me that and told myself that if Cliff was intimidated, then I should be terrified. At first, Cliff, like me, wondered whether the studio community would accept him. I watched as Cliff introduced himself to everyone, made friends, and demonstrated he was committed to learn and support others in that effort. He saw the depth and sincerity of support that existed and soon became a critical member of the tribe.

In time, I discovered that if Cliff was not working or sleeping, he was happily dancing. He was a student of steps and moves and generous with his time and knowledge with other less-advanced members of the tribe. As a surgeon, he knew the value of getting the procedure down correctly and practicing it over and over. As a musician, he had an ear for the beat and could time his step with the accuracy of a finely tuned clock. When it came time to perform, no man was better dressed. Like Jonas, Cliff became a great resource for me, whether I was struggling with my bow tie, remembering a name, or needing advice on how best to execute the male lead in a right turn in the waltz.

The dance gap between Natalie and Mike was considerable when they first met. Mike didn't mention his secret dance lessons to Natalie until years after he'd begun. They did take the necessary dance lessons for their wedding dance and then put the dance shoes away. For the next ten years, Mike's career required considerable travel; they paid down student loans and dancing was not in their budget. Natalie would suggest on occasion that they go dancing, but Mike always hesitated. Finally, Mike suggested to Natalie that he would go dancing with her on one condition: that they take lessons together. Mike knew it would take years to catch up with his disco-loving wife, but he was ready. And he had just enough experience from his clandestine lessons to know the frustration that lay ahead.

As married men with more dance-experienced spouses, Mike and I talked about our struggles with concurrently learning to dance and learning to lead our wives. We both knew that male students were far more likely to abandon dance lessons than females, and among married men the casualty rate was higher. Mike suggested that it would be useful for our wives to be required to play the role of leader in a few group dance classes. I agreed, but the odds of a dance studio adapting their approach to the specific needs of men like us were slim. We saw the role of the male lead as comparable to the driver of a car; sometimes there is traffic or bad weather. The man must set the pace and direction for his partner, keep the beat and, when it was crowded, protect his partner from collisions.

For a married man, leading a spouse who is a more experienced dancer is more complicated than leading other female dance partners. In those circumstances dancing needs to find its place within the context of the spousal relationship. The fact that the dance lesson conversation goes home with a married couple every night does not make it easier. In dance lessons, the male leader is taught that the female follower, spouse or not, should subordinate herself to the male lead. Only one person can drive the car. However, both Mike and I were married to strong-minded partners who were quick to offer unfiltered opinions about our dancing and slow to accept their role as followers. We needed to adapt what we were taught in dance class to the reality of life off the dance floor.

My own initial confusion about the roles of leaders and followers and males and females on the dance floor taught me that I needed to be careful about dance role assumptions. My blunder occurred at a Thursday night studio party. I had decided it was time to step up my dance game. The moment had come to demonstrate to Melissa that I had mastered what she had taught me. I spotted her, walked quickly across the floor, tapped her on the shoulder, smiled, and asked her to dance. Melissa replied politely. "Not now, Dan. Maybe you could dance with another student?"

Melissa turned her head back to the woman with whom she was conversing. Wow, that was a bummer I thought. After I got my nerve up to ask her to dance, I was rejected by my instructor. I wondered if I, a leader, had broken some aspect of ballroom dance etiquette? Did I embarrass her? Maybe she had more important people to dance with that night?

Melissa's rejection stuck with me the next day. That was not a good sign. My old self was telling me I was not at fault, Melissa was. She had encouraged me to dance with everyone and yet she had said no to me. Did she have a double standard? I felt a student shouldn't be treated as I had been that evening. Still I was surprised at myself. My new voice, the male student dance voice, wondered why I was so worked up. Rejection on the dance floor shouldn't be that big a deal, particularly for a beginner dancer. There could be several reasons Melissa said no. I should not assume her intent. I told myself I needed to let it go. I decided not to mention my feelings to anyone until I'd had a direct conversation with her.

At my next lesson, I approached Melissa and asked if we could talk. I asked if she found me a high-maintenance student and she said that she didn't, and looked at me quizzically. I then explained to her that when I had asked her to dance the week before, and she suggested I ask another student, I was upset. I didn't ask her to dance often at parties, but I was challenging myself that night. I went on to say that I had thought about the experience, and I wasn't sure I wanted to dance with her anymore. By the look on her face, I could tell she was surprised and hurt. She replied that sometimes she needed to play the role of leader and she had just asked a woman to dance when I approached.

At that stage of my dance education, I didn't understand what Melissa meant when she said she had to play the role of male leader. I asked her for an explanation. She mentioned there are usually more women than men at the dance parties so female instructors, like herself, often play the dance role of male leaders and ask females who had not been asked to dance. That was part of her job. She asked me if I wanted to talk to Kristen, her boss, about my disappointment or switch to another instructor. I said no, and that I felt it was a matter between the two of us.

I needed to think. Until that moment, I was not aware of the multiple roles female instructors played at dance parties. My male ego led me to question Melissa's motives. I was so naïve and sensitive about dance that I had acted like a jerk. I needed to accept the reality that rejection on the dance floor, intended or unintended, was part of dance life. Part of me wished I could erase the entire conversation. Another part of me said talking to Melissa face to face that night was a valuable lesson. I extended my left arm, looked at her, and said, "Let's forget this conversation and dance."

As we started to dance, the tension in my body eased. No doubt, my instructor sensed it as well. I reminded myself that learning and adapting to new cultures had its ups and downs. I had made a mistake in judging another person's intentions. In less than a minute, I had gone from being upset with Melissa to being upset with myself. That night, I chose to ask Melissa to dance to heal a misunderstanding. The dance felt good.

I had been fortunate to encounter a group of men like Jonas, Cliff, Mike, Ramsey, and Mathias. I could talk to them not only about dance steps and technique, but about how they felt. I had learned much from them. Later that evening Jonas was holding court. He loved to chat in the shoe room or on the dance floor perimeter and make small talk.

Dance provided Jonas a level of joy that only his dance-addict friends understood. When I asked Jonas why he danced, I got the sense there was nothing else in life that he would rather be doing. His mischievous eyes lit up, and I knew there was no short answer. Jonas told me that he loved every aspect of ballroom dance; the social parties, the lessons, performing in front of an audience, watching others perform, talking to the instructors, and meeting new dance students. He loved leading a woman in dance, connecting with them, and moving to the beat. I had reached a point in my dance journey where I understood Jonas's answer. I wondered how I might answer the question I asked him in a few years. I knew that answer would depend on what I could learn from my dance partners and how they would help me defeat the dragon. There were some things only women can teach men about dance.

Chapter Eight

The Joy of Dance

It was party time, and I made another mistake. Weeks after my wrong-way tango dance with Eileen and my more recent mishap with Melissa the instructor, I executed my first perfect chest bump. I was dancing the hustle with a frequent partner. In hindsight, for a male beginner, the hustle is a chest-bump accident waiting to happen. Melissa Agrimanakis, alias Melissa the dancer, as we called her, had arrived at the studio shortly after me. She was new to ballroom dancing, but you'd never guess it. She had spent a good part of her life in ballet, wanted to learn the waltz and tango, and had the strength and poise to do them well. I classified her as a "committed one" the day she walked in the door.

The hustle is a high-energy disco dance, popular in the seventies, open to personal interpretation. Melissa preferred the classic smooth dances in ballroom, but she seldom said no to a dance, even if she was not familiar with it. The basic idea in the hustle is for the leader to step directly toward his partner as he holds her hands down and slightly out and close to her waist, and then, at the last moment, swivel around her. That night, I didn't get around Melissa; she was defenseless and our chests collided. It happens. We both claimed responsibility for the frontal collision, laughed, and got back to dancing. I was the leader, and I think my step was off-beat. Fortunately, I have not experienced a chest bump in the hustle since.

During the day, Melissa was a physical therapist at Spaulding Rehabilitation Hospital in Boston. She helped people regain the use of their bodies. At night, she used her own body to dance. Her family came from Greece, and she had fond memories of family weddings and Greek folk dancing. Whenever I watched her practice with her instructor, I saw the parallel between her day job and dance. She completed a serious body stretch routine before she walked on the dance floor. Her body strength was evidence of a daily dedication to physical conditioning. She always had a smile on her face and her upper body frame never changed as she danced. She trusted her body on the dance floor, controlled her emotions, and focused on the dance one hundred percent. Later that same night, I asked Melissa whether she was addicted to dance and she answered:

"Yes, I'm addicted, but dance is a positive force in my life. In dance, I must temporarily give up control of myself, my freedom, to learn a new ballroom dance. I find that difficult to do; however, each time I give up that control, I know I will work hard to regain it. I will learn to perform the new dance and, in the process, become free again. Freedom on the dance floor is my reward. Ballroom dance keeps challenging me to express my freedom in different ways. That is my addiction."

Melissa's perspective on dance has stayed with me. Freedom may be the single most important asset a person possesses, yet there are times when we give it up to become free again. I understood the thought but, until Melissa said it, I had never thought of dance as a vehicle to express personal freedom. After listening to Melissa, I realized the depth of my own addiction. At times, for a few moments, dance had the power to make me forget everything, focus on the music, and move my body. I wanted to learn to harness that power.

The night of the chest bump, I did something else. For the first time, I danced with every female in the room. There were moments, depending on my partner or the dance, when I sensed the presence of the dragon, but I kept my focus on the music. One young lady I danced with was from Saudi Arabia and a short-timer. She was visiting her sister for two weeks and wanted to spend every spare moment learning to dance. Language was a challenge for us, but we connected. When I asked her to dance a foxtrot, she nodded and said two words in English "no experience." I found myself explaining the dance with body movements to her, and she trusted me to lead her on the dance floor. That was a new experience for me. I was giving back to a beginner what so many dancers had given to me.

For some time, I suspected several female tribe members knew there was a Dance Dragon in my head even though I'd never spoke of him. Lola was among them and kept me on the right path as I struggled. Whenever I grunted or sighed while dancing, she seemed capable of interpreting the sounds, whether they came from frustration, embarrassment, or rare moments of satisfaction. Her remedies varied from verbal encouragement, to advice, a laugh, or a simple nod. She understood why men like me grunted when they danced.

As a behavioral health nurse at a community hospital in Cambridge, Massachusetts, Lola knew addiction, both the good and the bad kind. I think she knew I was addicted to dance before I did. At night, Lola switches gears from nursing to dancing, but she never stops helping people. Kindness is part of her DNA. Lola has been dancing since she was born and planned to dance, as she said, "until the money runs out. " I didn't know how much money Lola had, but I did worry that her feet might wear out before the money. She was the only child of African-American parents, and she told me whenever she heard music she had to dance, even if it was by herself. Her body could not resist the power of music. Lola gladly accepted the pain in her feet to experience the joy of dancing. When I probed her one night on the importance of dance in her life, she replied:

"I believe the secret to a good life is keeping mentally and physically active, spiritually engaged and having a strong support group. Dance has provided me much of what I need in life. I learn something from every instructor and every group class I take. I dance with students and find something good in each person. When the music goes on, dance just takes over my body. I feel the dance and leave the studio physically exhausted. "

If dancing were a religion, Lola would be one of the saints. When you watch Lola dance, there is no tension in her body. She is full of joy and in sync with herself, the music, her partner, and her god. Somehow the music goes into her head and comes out through her body in the form of fluid body movement. I wanted to understand how she does that and what it feels like.

One day I asked Lola for the secret to joy on the dance floor. The focus of her message was different than anyone else I had posed the question to. She didn't talk to me much about steps, technique, posture, the beat, or smiling. She told me I needed to let go of everything in my head and find the feel of the dance in my body and soul. I felt like young Luke Skywalker listening to Obi-Wan Kenobi as he tried to comprehend the Force. I had no idea what Lola was talking about. I was a guy still working on his basic dance steps. But as the months turned into a year, things changed. I experienced brief moments when my mind was turned off and my body was free to express itself, and my soul was at peace with the world. For Lola, the feel of the dance was the equivalent of dance heaven, and she knew how to get there. For me the feel of the dance was still an unpredictable experience that rarely occurred, but, when it did, it was joy. The feeling did not last long enough for me to fully grasp it. It was but a sample of what could be. And, like a dream, I could not remember how to find it again when I woke up.

"Dan, do you realize you are doing the cha-cha?" Jane, a frequent dance partner who I first met in a cha-cha class with Elena, asked in a slightly startled voice. Jane was right. When the song started, I was dancing a swing and then suddenly I was dancing a cha-cha. Sometimes my body acted on its own and changed steps even while I kept the beat. It was as if my body was trying to connect directly to the music free of any interference from my brain. It was a weird sensation. After ten to fifteen seconds, my consciousness might return, tell me to snap out of it, and take me back to the original track. My body had been in pursuit of the feel of the dance. Melissa and dance partners who knew me made light of my behavior and told me it was no big deal. They could follow me. I could never tell whether they were being kind or honest.

When my body switched dances mid-song with strangers the reaction was more dramatic. Such behavior confused the follower who expected me, as a leader, to stick to the same dance. My partner might look at me as if they weren't sure what had just happened and were often at a loss for words. Their body movement stalled and sent me a message. I would then snap back to the original dance. I usually apologized when the dance was over, but they left bewildered.

The increasing tendency of my body to ignore my brain and let the music take over was a sign of progress. While I had not yet reached a point where I totally trusted my body, I was experimenting. Luke Skywalker would understand. Dancing was different from skiing or running. When I reached a natural high in those activities, I turned off my mind, drifted onto a cloud, and set my own pace. In dancing, the music—not the dancer—set the pace, and I had to follow the beat. Plus, I had a partner to lead.

Christina Ehlert was among the "committed ones". Like Lola, Christina was born with the urge to dance, though not in Boston, but in Siberia, over five thousand miles away. Christina was pursuing a graduate degree, and she wanted to learn everything she could about ballroom dance while she was in Boston. She told me that, as a young girl, whenever she heard music, she had to move her body to express her feelings. Christina grew up doing Russian peasant dances with her mother. When she was twelve, she moved to Bavaria, Germany. Within a few years, some of her new friends from traditional German families started to prepare for their introduction to society at formal balls. Her friends needed to learn many dances including the Viennese Waltz. At first, Christina hesitated to get involved in ballroom, but her friends kept encouraging her. Once she'd attended a few events, she discovered she loved the challenge of learning new dances.

The first time I saw Christina in a group class, she stood out. She was self-confident, and approachable, and had the body and posture of a dancer. My reaction as I approached her was to pull up my rib cage, pull my shoulders back, and make sure my head was up. Good posture was contagious in dancing. If my dance partner had good posture, I became more conscious of my own. My gut told me this woman was polite but serious about her dancing. Christina seemed to be at every group class and party and was taking private lessons as well. One day, in the spirit of making good social dance conversation, I asked Christina whether she had a favorite dance. She told me she didn't have one.

What Christina liked about dancing was that, with each new dance, she became a different person on the dance floor. She loved the tango because it forced her to be strong, fierce, and sharp. She did the waltz because it required her to be graceful. When she did a Latin dance like the salsa, she had fun and let herself go. Every time she danced, it meant she had to play the role of a different person, and that is what she loved about ballroom.

I did not know how Christina would evaluate herself as a dancer, but from my perspective she seemed equally comfortable dancing a samba, a foxtrot or a polka. She was fearless, wanting to try any dance and willing to learn them all. Her perspective on the cultural origins, different moods and personalities that a distinct dance required reminded me how global ballroom dance was.

Months after I met her, when Christina was getting ready to return to Europe, I asked her what made for a good dance partner regardless of where she danced. She told me that dance tested each of us and had a lot to do with trusting your partner, male or female. She wanted men to trust her on the dance floor and Christina liked men who could dance and whom she could trust. "Dance lets me know who people are. It also helps me learn my own limits and where I can go. "

I had heard Christina say the word "trust" several times in our conversation. She set a high bar. Christina reminded me of the tangolistas in Kapka Kassabova's book and the "mad ones" in my own studio. Christina wanted to experience ballroom, and, I suspect, life, as much as she could. Dance, for Christina, required a mutual understanding between the partners. She has danced with enough men to know that not every leader shared her passion to learn and grow as a dancer and that was okay. Her preference was to dance with men truly committed to dance, who could lead her on the dance floor.

I understood the distinction Christina was making. As a group, the partners we dance with over time, male or female, impact our motivation and help make us better dancers. She wanted to dance with leaders who were committed to learning and improving as well as having fun. Her message stuck with me. I did not know yet what my limits were in dance. However, I did know, both in my words and actions, I had to commit myself more to the joy and struggle of learning to find out.

Eileen and I were eating dinner a few nights after my conversation with Christina when a Leonard Cohen song called *Take This Waltz* came on Pandora. Cohen had a deep powerful voice and was part singer, poet and philosopher; for the latter reasons, he reminded us of Bob Dylan. Eileen and I had participated in a group waltz lesson a few weeks before, and the song led us to a conversation on what we had learned. We decided to dance to Cohen's song and test our memories.

We moved around our condo floor as we did a waltz. The song was long and the beat was fast. We had a good time, gave each other some feedback and then relaxed. We were learning to dance together and help each other. Somehow the lyrics, the music and Cohen's voice helped us focus just on the dance. I felt the feel of the dance for a few brief moments. The dragon was far away.

The more I danced the more I came to understand the relationship between myself and dance. I knew my brain was wired differently from that of other students, and there was a dragon somewhere in my head. I also knew that most of the women I danced with, regardless of their level, accepted that. It was okay for me not to be a great dancer. The important thing was to show up and be prepared to play the game as best you could. I wanted to speed up the pace of learning or change my approach, but I did not yet know how.

One day I found myself talking to Bobbi, a doctor in the Boston area who, along with her husband, Francis, had started taking dance lessons a few months after me. Bobbi asked me how often I came to the studio and what my approach was to learning . I told her I showed up three or four times a week and that my approach was to keep experimenting, as I had not found a preferred path or a short cut.

Francis was a computer-language expert and worked in Washington D. C. during the week, so the couple took lessons together on Fridays and Saturdays. Bobbi had done some dancing as a teenager but Francis was new to dancing. Francis was one of those men who, like me, had avoided dance his whole life. He told me he'd found dancing terrifying as a young man in rural Wisconsin. We bonded immediately. Bobbi and Francis were trying to figure out the best approach to learning as a couple, something Eileen and I struggled with as well. The dance gap between us was simply too great. Bobbi described herself as an experimental learner while Francis searched for patterns in dance and thought like an engineer. I mentioned to Bobbi that other men that I had met at the studio had engineering or science backgrounds and seemed to approach learning like Francis, but I was hardly an expert. I then asked her about experimental learning.

Bobbi's comment on being an experimental learner made me realize that this type of learning was the path I had taken most often in life. It was not necessarily the most efficient way to learn, but it was effective. I often needed to engage myself in the experience first, then analyze, adapt and try again. At a swim lesson, I remembered the lifeguard talking about finding a rhythm for breathing he then had us practice. I did not pay much attention to his message until one day in a swim race I ran out of breath and swallowed a considerable amount of salt water. I finished last and then reflected on the experience. The same was true of skiing. I had to fall or ski out of control into the woods several times before I learned how to control my speed. In dance, maybe I needed to experiment more, make more mistakes. I began to think about taking bigger risks in the dance world. An absurd thought came to mind, from which I quickly retreated.

When I first committed to take lessons, I promised myself I would never do a solo dance performance in front of a large crowd. That would be crazy. I would focus only on social dancing when there were other couples on the dance floor. Yet, a few months back, after significant pressure from Melissa, I had put my toe in the performance water and did a short waltz solo at the studio in front of a small, friendly crowd. I held onto Melissa while she mostly back-led me. It was a dance I wanted to forget. I never watched the video. Melissa no doubt sensed my fear that night but pointed out that there are some things in life you need to experience to understand. I could not refute her logic but neither could I rationalize inflicting that much pain on myself again.

I was desperate to learn so I put my better judgment and fear aside and decided to talk to Melissa. We had a thoughtful discussion about experimentation on the dance floor and how I could improve my learning. She offered a few modest suggestions, which made sense, but I knew their impact on my dance development would also be modest. It was the slow but steady approach. I asked Melissa what she would do if she were in my situation. She replied she would challenge herself. She paused and waited for my reaction.

Melissa was daring me to push myself. It was my move, and I was trapped as if in a chess game. I knew her story and how she had challenged herself to become the dancer she was. I hesitated for a few seconds, knowing what her answer would be if I asked her how I could challenge myself. I finally asked the question, and Melissa answered with a happy face that I must do a solo performance. She said this time it would be different. This time I must take the lead on the dance floor. I nodded and smiled, realizing, if I did it, I would either accelerate my learning curve or make a big fool of myself.

Chapter Nine

The Buttons

I was dressed in black, like Zorro, but without the sword and mask for self-defense. I stared at the floor as I waited for the music to begin. My non-dancing male friends would never understand why I put myself in this situation. I was alone. Melissa was far away on the other side of the floor. I was focused on performing my first tango solo at the studio in front of the tribe. I must play the role of the confident macho male and lead my partner across the dance floor.

The history of the tango varies depending on whom you ask. Most stories suggest the dance became popular in the 1880s around the brothels of Buenos Aires. There, long lines of poor, uneducated men, mostly immigrant workers from Europe, waited for their turn with a woman of the night. The brothel owners often provided musical entertainment, drinks and a female dancer to keep their potential customers busy.

The origins of the tango were about as earthy and male as a dance can get. The basic steps involved walking with a swagger, and the dance protocol required close body contact. To understand the dance you only need to imagine the smell of warm body sweat and sour breath and the desires of lonely men. The men, some, no doubt, with unbuttoned shirts, unwashed and sweaty, would take turns dancing and making body contact with partially dressed prostitutes. The world of poor working-class men in Buenos Aires in the 1880s was full of violence, drugs, sex, and alcohol. The tango reflected their sadness, their emotional and physical desires, and their hopes for a better life.

But there is another aspect to the tango. Over time the dance's popularity ascended to the wealthy class of Argentina who, in turn, took the dance to Paris, London, and New York. As the dance moved up in society, so did the rules of dress code, language, and hygiene. The men who danced the tango were now "gentlemen", bathed, groomed, and articulate, dressed in tuxedos and bow ties. They no longer carried knives in their waistbands. The women were fastidious, hair done up, dressed in elegant evening gowns. Close, but gentler, body contact remained essential to the dance.

The best way to understand and feel high-society tango is to go to YouTube and search tango dances in movies. Words alone cannot capture the feeling that the music and body movement create. The movie *Easy Virtue*, set in England in the Roaring Twenties, portrays a tango dance scene with Jessica Biel and Colin Firth. *Scent of a Woman* has a tango scene in present-day New York City with Al Pacino, playing the role of a blind man, dancing with Gabrielle Anwar. These performances depict social classes and cultures that are far removed from the slums of Buenos Aires in the 1880s.

My goal that evening was not to compete with the male leads in these movies but to be inspired by them. A great tango dance is a powerful emotional experience for both the dancer and the audience. For a social dancer with some basic degree of competence, the dance can be fun, provided you don't take yourself too seriously. Because the tango is raw, earthy, and physically intimate, the dancers must project some of that character in the dance. I arrived at the studio in a black shirt, black slacks, and an untied red bow tie around my open collar. Melissa had suggested the day before that I also unbutton the top four buttons of my shirt and partially roll up my sleeves. The idea behind the buttons, sleeves, and untied bow tie was to suggest our dance was spontaneous, that it was late in the evening and I had abandoned not only my formal attire but also some of my gentlemanly ways. On the continuum of primitive male to gentleman, I needed to come across as more macho and passionate than my usual self.

I accepted Melissa's advice on everything but unbuttoning the four top buttons of my shirt. I have often been confused about leaving shirt buttons unbuttoned in social situations. My old "straight Anglo" voice was in a battle with my new "let loose and learn to dance" inner voice. I remembered a conversation about men and buttons with Viviana, a fearless young dance partner with Latino roots who enjoys the studio and its community, and brought her energy to every dance. I had sought her perspective on buttons a few weeks earlier. She told me, "Buttons can be an issue with men. Aside from the cost of ballroom dancing, the young men in my office resist ballroom dancing because of the thought of dancing with most of the buttons on their shirt undone. The way men are dressed on "Dancing with The Stars" is a turn-off to some of them. It is not who they are. "

Viv had a quick wit and keen insight, and I valued her opinion. I was trying to determine my own dance identity. I was comfortable with colored tee shirts; formal wear and open buttons were new to me. I never mentioned the Dance Dragon to Viv, but I had no doubt she knew such dragons exist in the minds of some men. I decided to probe why Viv danced and how she felt.

"The dance bar in my family was set very high," she told me. "My mother was born in Columbia and my father in Argentina. They are both very good dancers. My cousins in Columbia taught me how to dance but I still work at feeling normal when I do rhythm dances with them. Dance is a big part of life in Columbia, much more so than in the United States. When I came to the studio I knew I had a cultural advantage over some students because I felt Latin music and dance in my body; it was part of me. " Viv lived in both the Latin and the Anglo dance world. She could have just danced to Latin music all night but, like Melissa the dancer, she chose to challenge herself and learn new dances. "I focused on learning the steps and how to become a good follower in non-Latin ballroom dances like the waltz and foxtrot. The music and the dance as well as the people around me impact when, if and to what degree I feel the dance. "

Viv understood that buttons matter for some males and she did not pass judgment on them. In her own way, Viv had told me that the feel of the dance would take time to evolve. Viv's message was common sense to herself but, for me, it was wisdom. As I waited for Melissa to practice, I thought about the buttons on my shirt and the fierce tango I hoped to do someday. As for that night, the bar I had set for myself was already high enough: just show up and finish the dance.

Melissa arrived in the practice area, walked up to me with a playful smile on her face and unbuttoned the second and third buttons on my shirt. She was testing me. When she started to move toward the fourth button, I gave her a look and shook my head. Without exchanging words, we agreed on the compromise. She was pushing me to dance with a style and attitude that fit Latin music. I appreciated her intent, but my limit that night was three undone buttons. I would think about four buttons the next time, after getting some input from my button consultant.

My dance performance lasted a minute and thirty seconds, and you can't find it on YouTube. We danced the tango to a song called *Pa'Bailar,* which is Spanish for "to dance. " The lyrics and the dance tell the story of a woman, played by Melissa, who wants to dance with a man, played by me, whose eyes had been tracking her moves all evening. The young woman wants to know who this man is and why he's stalking her. I looked across the room at the woman and, with my eyes, silently asked her to dance. With her head held high, her shoulders back and chin out, and with the slightest of nods, the woman accepted my request.

As the dance began, I moved across the floor with my head up and knees bent in a slightly crouched position. My chest was pushed out and my arms were away from my body and taut as if I was carrying a bucket of paint in each arm. Melissa was moving to the music in a semi-circle twenty feet away from me. She moved like a young panther on the prowl. We looked at each other with fake disinterest and then I stepped toward her, and silently, with no sign of emotion, invited her to join me if she dared. She accepted, moved very close to me, and I placed my right hand firmly on her back. I glanced away from her face with macho indifference.

As man and woman, we moved quickly around the floor as the tango music filled the air. At one point, just before I was to lead her through a swivel, I looked in Melissa's eyes. She appeared to be in a trance-like state, focused on the music and silently telling me she trusted me to lead her through the rest of the dance. I moved my body forward, counterclockwise, in slow motion, so she could adjust her balance and start to swivel. I concentrated on trying to feel her body movement and weight shift in sync to the music. At the end of the sequence, I led her into a double tango close. I was slightly off balance but recovered. We both acted as if nothing had gone askew.

After that off-balance move, either because I recovered, or because Melissa didn't acknowledge it, I got back on track. Melissa made me look good that night. She was concentrating on building my confidence as a leader one button at a time. If I made a mistake, it was not a big deal. I thought about my conversation with Christina Ehlert about how dance helps us understand who we are and how important it is to have a partner on the dance floor you can trust. That night I experienced the exchange of trust that ballroom dance performance requires.

Performance dancing differs from social dancing in that all your steps and moves are choreographed in advance. Judges watch you and evaluate every aspect of your performance. The audience watches your body movement and chemistry with your partner. You practice the performance until your muscle memory transcends real time and you follow the music. Performance dancing is comparable to being on stage in a play. You must keep going even if you screw up your lines or, in this case, your moves. If you think too much before you move your body, then is too late. If you move your body ahead of the music, then you are moving too soon.

The night I did the tango, my mind did not fast-forward ahead of the music and my muscle memory stayed true to the pace and sequence of my dance. I was patient and nervous at the same time. I graded myself a C plus. I needed to work on my body movement, dance the tango closer to my partner, and put more energy and expression into my dance. I had listened to *Pa'Bailar* at least fifty times over the previous weeks and counted the beat out in my head often. I had practiced aspects of that dance with Melissa and by myself for many hours.

The tango video scenes I had watched on YouTube helped, as did thinking about the roots of the dance in Buenos Aires. Like an amateur golfer watching the Masters tournament, or an aspiring young baseball player imagining playing in the world series, a dance student needs to dream of what is possible, even if the logical side of their brain tells them it is impossible.

What I did that night was, for me, extraordinary. I had challenged the Dance Dragon in my head and did not back off. In the world of performance ballroom dancing, my beginner-level tango was, at best, ordinary. For me, it was less about the dance and more about the risk I had been willing to take on the dance floor and my battle with the Dance Dragon. I had to compete with my "old self" and rather than allow feelings of awkwardness, embarrassment, or frustration to dominate my thinking, I focused on the music and the dance, nothing else.

After my dance, two men who introduced themselves as Steve and Peter asked me how I felt on the dance floor. "Were you nervous or self-conscious?"Peter asked.

"I was both. Several times, my mind was lost in a black hole for a second or two but my body kept moving. "

The men told me they had come to watch Steve's girlfriend perform with her male instructor. They could never learn to dance, let alone perform, both men told me in slightly different ways. Steve asked me why I did it. I explained that performance was an immense struggle for me but it was the best way for me to learn. Peter asked me if I enjoyed dancing. I laughed as I was not sure any one word reflected the total feeling within me at that moment. I surprised myself when I answered that, yes, I did enjoy parts of my dance. Steve wondered whether I would do it again, and I found myself saying yes. I now knew I could improve, so I would push myself again. Steve and Peter looked at me as if I were possessed. I looked at them and saw men who feared dance.

Chapter Ten

The Avoiders

I know the fear of dance because I had lived it. Yet, I had just completed a solo performance and, rather than walk out the door, embarrassed or frustrated, I wanted to do it again. Steve and Peter continued the conversation and wanted to know when and why I took up dancing. I gave them my now standard sixty-second answer.

I told them I had made a fool out of myself several times on the dance floor when I was young so I stopped trying to learn. That was my mistake. As the years went by, the more I avoided dance, the harder it became to try to learn. I convinced myself that the problem was my lack of ability, not my fear of making a fool of myself. To make matters worse, my male friends often supported that point of view, a view they themselves often used as their rationale for dance avoidance. When my daughter decided to get married, I knew I had to dance, even though it was a struggle. I was always envious of the joy of dancing that I saw in other people. In the process of getting ready for the wedding dance, something happened inside me; a curiosity, an urge, a feeling, and I could not go back to my danceless life until I figured out what that feeling was. I joined a studio tribe to learn more about dance and myself.

Steve and Peter smiled in silence as I explained my conversion to dance. They were so inquisitive about my journey that I wondered if they thought I had an addiction or that I was a "mad one. " I never mentioned the existence of the Dance Dragon to them, as that would only confirm that I was mad in multiple ways. Instead, I said that someday I hoped to see them on the dance floor. Steve and Peter did not respond.

Conversations with male dance-avoiders like Steve and Peter helped me understand how dragons operated. Male avoiders were often intensely curious about dance and asked me lots of questions. Then suddenly the questions would stop, and I could sense fear, self-doubt, and perhaps even a dragon, within them. Occasionally an avoider crossed the line and asked about instructors and lessons. That took courage. If they gave into the fear I knew, as in my case, the dragon would only become stronger. Avoiders with dragons needed to be careful if they wanted to be converted. They must find an instructor who understood dragons. Otherwise they would most likely fail.

Later that evening I was dancing with Ashley and shared the conversation I'd had with Steve and Peter. I asked Ashley how she convinced dance avoiders to dance. Ashley was, at the time, a twenty-year-old student at Northeastern University, personable, and a great dancer. Like many colleges in the Boston area, there was a ballroom dance club at her school and they held dance parties. More young women showed up than young men. One of her roles as an active club member was to encourage men to come to the dance parties.

"It isn't as easy as you think, Dan, to get a college-aged boy to dance. Ultimately, I need to lead them on a bit. Since they usually have a strong desire to meet girls, I let them know atballroom dance parties they can meet girls and be close to them. Sometimes I joke and say to them where else can you put your hands on a beautiful young woman you never met before? Sometimes, at a dance, a boy will slowly drop his hands down my back and keep going. At some point, I need to stop him. I smile, reach for their hand, and raise it back up. Most of the time that works. If it happens a second time, I do the same but I don't smile. That is just the way some boys are. In the beginning of the school year, a fair number of boys show up at our dance parties, but as the year progresses most of them don't come back. "

All I could do was smile and nod at Ashley. There was truth and humor in her story. My guess was that the real reasons males did not come back to Ashley's college dance parties were either that they felt foolish on the dance floor or they were not ready to make a real effort to learn to dance.

A week later, I asked Melissa during a warm-up if she thought men were afraid to dance because they did not want to make fools out of themselves. Melissa replied that men who truly fear dancing never come into the studio. The hardest thing was to walk in the door. The men who were willing to try to learn usually found enough support to keep at it for a month or two and then the experience of dancing motivated some of them to keep working at it.

I knew from the time I walked through the studio door that making a fool out of myself in front of my instructor was necessary if I wanted to learn. Melissa recalled one man who left before the lesson even started. The fellow had said he thought his lesson would be in a private room where no one else could see him. Melissa explained the studio was not designed with private rooms in mind and in fact large dance floors were preferable for most dances.

While Melissa was surprised by this man's behavior, I was not. I had talked to men who stopped taking lessons because they had been frustrated with their inability to learn or embarrassed about making fools of themselves. I will always remember Paul, a well-accomplished man in life, and an excellent dance student. He could hear the beat and had good posture from the day he arrived at the studio. One night, when he finished a studio dance solo to applause, he walked by me with a pained look on his face. He kept walking all the way to the door, opened it, and left. I never saw him again. Several weeks later, I met his wife on the street. She had been out of town during his performance. She told me how upset he was with his performance and that he'd decided to stop dancing. Men can become very emotional when they perceive they look bad on the dance floor, just as women can become upset with a man who will not try to dance.

When I asked Jeff Cameron, one of the few male "mad ones" at the studio, about men who avoided dancing, I heard a different perspective. Jeff, who has worked hard at becoming a very competent male ballroom dancer, said he was baffled by the mindset of some male dance avoiders. For years, he worked on Wall Street and spent his weekends with the same crowd on the golf course. Jeff answered my question with a question. "Why would a successful Wall Street businessman with a supportive female partner attend a golf club dance party and want to sit at the table all night while other men approached his female partner and asked for a dance? I can understand not wanting to look like a fool on the dance floor, but sitting by yourself while your partner dances away the night with other men might make you look like a bigger fool. "

The logic in Jeff's question was clear, but he had been dancing since high school. It is hard to judge the intensity of another man's discomfort or pain when he cannot dance. Male avoiders do not want to choose between looking like a fool for avoiding a dance or going onto the floor and making a fool of themselves trying. As a successful dance-avoider, I had rarely been caught in such situations. But one night several years before Caroline's wedding, I got trapped at a party and was virtually dragged onto the dance floor.

I'd been at an annual community black-tie event, which raised money for youth and elderly neighborhood programs. The chairperson of the event was well-known, kind, outgoing, fun-loving, and a true believer in the cause. She was also an outrageously provocative dresser and blessed with the physical assets that made her one of the most attractive women in Boston. Her dress that evening exceeded her reputation, and any direct conversation with her that night made more than a few men stutter.

I, too, believed in the cause, was on the event committee and had done my best to raise money. That night, as the band was about to play a song, the chairperson caught me off-guard. I was sitting at my table by myself when she suddenly appeared, grabbed both my hands, and insisted I dance with her. It was her way of thanking me for my support. For me, it would take months to recover from that dance. I was frozen with embarrassment, and when the music started, I assumed everyone was watching. I became so flustered that somehow my red cummerbund snapped and fell to the dance floor. I was grateful for the soft lights as my face, no doubt, was as red as my cummerbund. The light-hearted comments from the crowd afterwards were well-intended and publicly I laughed them off. How I felt inside was another matter.

Several months after my tango, I met a male dragon-slayer. I was in the aisle seat at the back of a plane on a flight from Los Angeles to Boston. My consulting assignment was over, and my mind was on dance. There was a very big man sitting next to me. He was much taller than me and weighed close to 250 pounds. He sat straight in his seat.

I am a "hunt-and-peck" typist. I usually stop after a few sentences and correct my work. My mind drifted and I wondered how the man managed to get his big body into such a small seat. His knees were squeezed against the seat in front of him. He looked straight ahead with his headphones on, apparently relaxed and content. Occasionally, I stopped pecking on the keyboard and stared into space, thinking. The man assumed I was taking a break and said he needed to use the bathroom. I stood up to let him pass and saw that he was quite fit and agile. When he returned to his seat, he smiled and asked me if I was a writer. I explained I was a novice, writing a few pages for what someday might be a book. He introduced himself as Kai. "What is your book about?" Kai inquired. I told him it was about the challenge a man faces learning to do something he avoided all his life and the people he meets who help him on his journey. My book is about ballroom dancing. I prepared myself for my usual conversation about men and dance and my sixty-second answer. I would be polite but I wanted to get back to writing. "I dance," Kai said. "I grew up in Hawaii, but along with most of my family I live now in Los Angeles. I have five sisters and together we own several restaurants. Whenever we can, we go out dancing. We dance to just about every type of music including swing, Latin, country, and ballroom. "

For the next few hours, we talked about men and dancing. I tried to imagine this big man on the dance floor doing a swing dance. He was raised in a small Hawaiian village overlooking the ocean. At first, his older sisters insisted he dance with them since they needed a male partner. They would teach Kai steps and he would improvise on his own. As the years went by, his younger sisters also required his presence. Most evenings after dinner, his sisters and friends would dance outside their home until dark. Kai reached a point when his body just moved to any music. He told me that dancing had become as effortless for him as swimming and surfing. I was jealous.

As a grown man, his sisters still asked him to dance, but now they told him he was among the best dancers in Los Angeles. He laughed when he told me this and explained he was no Michael Jackson. He saw himself as a good social dancer and knew their compliments were a set-up. They wanted him to talk to their husbands and boyfriends and help their men become comfortable on the dance floor. They themselves had not been that successful. They thought a man who danced well might have a better outcome with other men. The men in his sisters' lives had a variety of reasons for avoiding dancing. Kai told me their stories. Some were convinced it was too late in their life to learn, they lacked rhythm, or they could not hear the beat. Several of them said they were too self-conscious or awkward. At one time or another, they all mentioned that the dance gap between themselves and his sisters was simply too much to overcome. But they also told Kai in various ways that they wanted to learn to make the women in their lives, his sisters, happy. I asked how he responded to that.

"I told them the truth; I was lucky to learn to move my body to music when I was a young boy. I understood how hard it would be for them to learn to dance now at their age. Dancing, like basketball, which several of them still played, takes considerable time to learn and they would get very frustrated at times. If they could play basketball or almost any sport they had rhythm. I told them if they wanted to learn to dance at initially they would feel like fools. They would have to deal with that. They joked with me about how uncoordinated I looked when I tried to shoot hoops. I told them how ridiculous I felt playing basketball with them. My explanation for being a big man who could not play the game was that no one in my village played basketball. I was raised in Hawaii and we surfed, swam, and fished. They told me as boys they never danced and they would try to learn. They also suggested to me it was never too late to learn to play basketball. "

The men made a deal. They would teach Kai basketball and he would teach them dance. They would not quit unless all six of them agreed. In effect, Kai agreed to make a fool of himself to level the playing field. He told his sisters they must be patient and provide honest feedback. Sugar-coating and false praise were not allowed. I realized that Kai had never taken a lesson in a dance studio.

Kai told me that the men practiced both dance and basketball, sometimes in a group and sometimes one-on-one. They become good friends in the process. Today, three of those the men are good dancers but two are still struggling. No one had quit. I asked Kai about his progress in basketball. He learned, in time, to run and dribble the ball at the same time and now has a net over his garage door. He shoots baskets by himself whenever he can. He needed his own struggle with basketball to better understand the struggle the men faced with his sisters.

When the plane landed, I asked Kai why he and his sisters enjoyed dancing so much.

"Dance keeps us connected to our roots and to each other. I told the men I taught that dance was important to my sisters for that reason and we would all welcome them joining us in that experience. They have, and my sisters are happy. "

I wished Kai many more dances with his sisters. The men Kai taught to dance were fortunate. They had an instructor who understood them and figured out how to overcome whatever fears, doubts or inhibitions existed in their heads. Kai was a dance dragon-slayer.

Chapter Eleven

The Dragon-Slayers

A good dance instructor can teach a man how to move his body, but only a dragon-slayer can recognize a man who is possessed by a dragon and help defeat it. I thought about the few dragon-slayers who had impacted my own dance life. They had accepted the existence of the dragon rather than make light of him. They knew they had to defeat the dragon in my head and free me from my doubts, fears or inhibitions before the music could ever take over my body and allow me to truly feel the dance.

Men with a dragon in their head are not easily recognized. They work hard at keeping the dragon a secret. These men often abandon dance before they are identified because they believe that there is no cure for their affliction. Unless a dance dragon has possessed you, the power of dragons can be hard to understand. In my early days at the studio, I kept my dragon a deep secret. Once or twice, I caught Elena giving me a strange look in a group class, as if she had figured it out, but she handled too many students to focus only on me. Over time, I dropped hints to the instructors, but only a few picked up on them. I never explicitly announced to anyone in the studio tribe that I had a dragon in my head.

Melissa Friebe, my instructor, was unusual. She was even-tempered, day in and day out. Patience could have been her middle name and was part of her DNA. She seldom talked about herself and, like most good instructors, was always focused on her student. When Melissa put the music on for the first dance in our lesson, she'd enthusiastically take quick steps to the computer, hit the button and, with her long stride, would be back before the music started.

"Are you ready, Melissa?" I'd say and she'd smile and nod. I'd raise my left arm and she'd extend her right arm outward. She would select the distance from me that was comfortable for her. I would close my right arm around her and place my right hand near her shoulder blade. I'd wait for the downbeat, which I sometimes missed, and the lesson would begin. I always felt connected to her energy, my mind was focused, and I was inspired to learn. This was the way I wanted to feel whenever I started a lesson. I knew that much about dance.

After my tango performance at the studio, I wanted to be a better dancer. However, for two months I avoided watching my tango video and just enjoyed the memories. I was taking a pause in my dance journey. When I finally decided to watch the video, it took me back to reality, and made me think of the Dance Dragon. In the video, I saw some progress in my dance, but my eyes were drawn to my weaknesses as I played the video again and again. I saw a man who still did not move his body well to the music. I needed to acknowledge why that was and fix the problem, which I knew was in my head. In sports, I moved with confidence. In dance, that was not the case. I would hesitate for a fraction of a second and then it was too late. The dragon still made me doubt myself, brought attention to my inhibitions, and made me fear dancing with better dance partners.

Melissa asked my opinion of the video. I told her I saw a man who was still closer to being a stiff than a dancer. I wanted to feel the music in my body all the time and be more expressive on the dance floor. I wanted to free my body from whatever was holding me back.

It was not just my words, but the intensity with which I said them, that resulted in Melissa giving me her "slow down and be patient" look. Melissa knew me well enough to read my frustration, whether it was in my voice, my words or my eyes. I knew her well enough to tell her exactly how I felt. The Dance Dragon was a cunning foe and to defeat him required that I allow Melissa to get into my head and expose any fears or inhibitions that were holding me back. I gave Melissa my honest thoughts because she listened, tried to understand my mindset, and was thoughtful about making recommendations she could deliver on. She never promised a quick fix.

Melissa reminded me I must focus on the positive aspects of my tango video. My posture and steps were generally good, and I had kept the beat most of the time. I had succeeded in making my dance persona somewhat aligned with the mood of the tango. As I listened to her, I could not disagree with those aspects of her assessment. However, I wanted to destroy the dragon, not coexist with him on the dance floor. At times, the battle with the Dance Dragon wore me down, and I became impatient with my progress.

Melissa put my own self-assessment in context. The fact that my dance focus had moved from steps and patterns to body movement was a new phase in my development. She committed to developing a new lesson plan to address that when I returned from a vacation I was about to take. As I left the studio, I thought about a conversation I had with Melissa many months ago.

I had been ready to quit dancing. I had taken too many dance lessons and reached a point where I felt that I was not making any more progress. The Dance Dragon was too strong for me to overcome. I told Melissa during our warm-up dance that day that I had my doubts about learning to dance, that I was frustrated and maybe I should move on in life. I didn't tell Melissa about the Dance Dragon.

Melissa did something she had never done before or since; she stopped dancing in the middle of a song. Melissa looked directly at me, took a deep breath, exhaled and said "Dan, you need to manage your expectations. You walked into the studio with no dance experience and no understanding of music. What did you expect? Learning to dance takes time. You need to be patient. " She spoke with such conviction that I realized there would be no further conversation. I stood still for about ten seconds listening to my inner self and fighting off the dragon. I raised my left hand to connect with Melissa's right, and started to dance again. I could feel the tension between us slowly evaporate. Melissa didn't ask me about the Dance Dragon that day. I sensed she knew and words were not necessary. In those ten seconds, I had changed my mind. I had achieved a small victory over the dragon and I was dancing with the dragon-slayer who was responsible for that victory.

My thoughts returned to the tango video. The tango was my first significant exposure to body movement. The dance required strong and precise upper and lower body movements while I maintained a solid upper-body frame. I did not appear to be either strong or precise in my movement in that video, and at key moments my timing was off. When I led with my arms rather than my core, I lost the feel and location of my partner's body and had to push or pull her to get us back on time. Other times, my body was too far away from my partner's and we could not move in sync. Melissa could have told me my weaknesses the night we performed, but often she waited for me to figure it out for myself.

Ironically, when I viewed the video, I was impressed that I could now see most of my mistakes. I had to lead with my core and eliminate any inhibitions about degrees of closeness on my part in the tango. I needed to be more aggressive in my role as leader no matter who my partner was. The tango is a dance of physical power and strength, yet it requires exceptional balance and body control. It would take many months of practice to get better. I knew that without a woman in my arms to practice with, I could not replicate the feeling of closeness, balance and body movement I needed to master. I needed to practice with female bodies in my arms. The Dance Dragon knew that as well.

When I returned from vacation, Melissa asked if I had done any dancing.

I told her I'd danced the tango basic on the grass with my friend Cindy one night in Maine. Eileen coached from the sidelines. I led with my core at times, slid my right leg forward between Cindy's legs, and let her pass close by me before I shifted my weight. At times, I felt as if I were on a balance beam. The difference was that there were two of us on the beam. I lost my balance on occasion, and we had our share of body contact. I did reasonably well that night and had Cindy's attention.

Another night, I went to a group samba lesson at a nearby dance studio. I lined up across from a woman who introduced herself as Erica. She elected to stand very, very close to me. I stood my ground, as it was her choice. I put my arm on her back and created some body pressure by leaning forward. Erica complimented me on how well our bodies connected. She told me that it was wonderful to dance so close to a male partner with a strong dance frame. I just nodded and had a flashback to my dances with Piera and her efforts to improve my dance frame and body closeness months before. I could feel the rhythm in Erica's body as we danced, and together the two of us found the beat and stayed on it.

The physical intimacy of dancing close with a total stranger like Erica awakened and impacted all my senses. When that happened, everything came together and made for a good dance. Our bodies sent messages to each other and those bodies instinctively drew their own conclusions. I realized again that night the importance of determining the right degree of closeness with each partner and how it allowed dancers to express and read each other's body movement. For students, closeness can be an adventure; for an instructor, closeness is part of their everyday job. Dancing with Erica was a reminder that while I needed to let the woman choose her distance, regardless of her choice, I could not be intimidated.

Melissa asked me to describe how those two dance experiences made me feel. I replied that I'd felt awkward, alive, connected, curious, and self-conscious all at the same time. My senses, and therefore my body, were engaged in the dance. I could feel the movement and location of my partner, and lead her with my core and legs. I was fortunate that Cindy, a friend, and Erica, a stranger, were open to my experimentation. I needed to take more chances and play my role as leader, realizing not every dance partner would be as forgiving.

Melissa and I started work on body movement and expression. It was new territory for me. With each new dance drill, I was initially tense, uptight, and unsure of myself. Melissa stopped frequently and would repeatedly say the word "relax" to loosen my arm, neck, and leg muscles and weaken the dragon's resistance. Melissa was, as always, patient but persistent with her drills. She was trying to help my body become loose, flexible, and tension-free through movement. The repetition would bore some men. One of Melissa's former students commented that she wore him down with her drills. I understood his perspective, as every student is different. In my case, I wanted repetition to wear down the Dance Dragon.

One day, we practiced extending my arms and hands inward and outward to the beat of the rumba and then the cha-cha. At first, it felt awkward to move both my feet and my arms to the same musical rhythm. I had never done it before. I also realized the more body parts I engaged with the music, the more essential timing became. The good news was I felt as if someone had just untied my arms. My arms were free to express themselves, and now I had to develop more muscle memory to the music. I was excited about more body movement but knew once again I needed to get better at following the beat.

Her name was Christine and we were in the yoga studio. The room had floor-to-ceiling mirrors, a great dance floor and a music system. As in yoga class, the lights were off, so the room was in semi-darkness. The room had one transparent wall, like the adjacent squash courts, so people walking by could stop and observe. Christine, my dance partner, was a born extrovert and an experienced performer. Dancing in a bubble, as people observed her, was not her concern, it was mine. My new self was on display.

What would you like to dance, Christine inquired? It was my first dance lesson with her. She had no idea what to expect. I suggested we start with a cha-cha and then a rumba. Both dances required considerable body movement. Christine did not back-lead me, nor did she count the beat. I was on my own. We danced for five or ten minutes. I tried to be conversational but knew Christine was evaluating my dancing. As expected, Christine asked for my own self-assessment first. I summed up how I had gotten started in ballroom, my experience to date with lessons and dance parties, and my two big concerns at the time: hearing the beat and moving more of my body to the music. When I talked about my music concerns and hearing the beat, Christine's eyes lit up. She suggested we listen to music together and focus on the beat. Christine then asked me to identify the downbeat or 1, and select what dance would work best with the beat of the music.

I was introduced to Christine at a dance party by her boyfriend, Kurt, a friend of mine from the advertising world and a drummer in a local band. Christine grew up around dance. Her mother taught ballroom, and all four of her grandparents played musical instruments; she majored in dance in college and then worked at Disneyland in Orlando in a mix of musical shows before returning to Boston for family reasons. Dance, not just ballroom, was her passion. Christine spent most of her time teaching children ballet but also taught private dance lessons to wedding couples and a few men I knew. Christine was familiar with my dance studio, as she once had worked there. and that was helpful. She was not interested in competing with them. She was interested in helping me become a better dancer.

On that first day, we barely danced. Mostly we talked about music and the beat and how rhythm directed our bodies to move at a certain tempo or pace. Christine asked me to clap my hand to the beat of a Michael Buble song called *The Way You Look Tonight.* It took less than a minute for me to prove I could not. We laughed and Christine asked me what else I could not do. I told her I didn't know how to ride a bike or jump rope. We laughed some more about my childhood and discovered we had grown up in the same area south of Boston and attended the same Catholic elementary school. We then put some music on and started to work on clapping.

We had the yoga studio to ourselves. Unlike a dance studio where other students might be present, we could switch the music as often as needed. I made some progress at clapping and then we talked about drums. We listened to music where the drum was dominant and I learned how the sound of the drum was often the instrument to find when you were searching for the "1", or downbeat, in a song. I often missed the first step in dance so the expression "I got off on the wrong foot" had taken on a new meaning for me. I wanted to become competent at finding the downbeat. I knew that it could take a few years.

Lessons with Christine were different from those at my dance studio. We did not follow a set agenda or curriculum. The clock was not ticking, and the length of the lessons varied. There was no floor traffic so it was easier to focus. In addition to music, we talked about dance, both social and performance, and the challenges of a male leader. We also talked about my self-doubt and inhibitions, and the moments of self-discovery and joy I experienced on the dance floor. We took it slow and easy; dance was not a race, she reminded me.

Occasionally someone came by the yoga studio for a workout, or we might have an audience of a few people passing by. We welcomed them. I became better at dancing in the presence of others. This club had been my home away from home for more than twenty years. People knew me as something of a jock, and now I was taking yoga and learning how to ballroom dance. The new me was evolving in my old environment. Christine understood both the male world from which I came, and where I was going. She was determined to help get me there, enjoy the journey, and slay the dragon along the way.

Christine told me to listen to the beat of the music in a song whenever and wherever I could. I should practice determining what dance I would do to the beat. If I was unsure I should send her an email with my best guess. She always responded and corrected me if I was wrong. When I was social dancing and could not find the beat, the first thing I did was to search for the drum. Christine's advice has stuck with me. Like Melissa and Kai, I started to hear her voice when she was not in the room. She had the voice of a dragon-slayer.

Chapter Twelve

Energizer Bunnies

We need energy to move our bodies. At a dance studio, the instructors are responsible for creating energy and movement. They provide the spark that starts us moving, and once they start, they never stop. They are the energizer bunnies of the dance world. When I first walked into the studio, I was amazed at the energy level of the instructors. The instructor needed energy for him or herself, but also had to energize an endless variety of students all day.

I started referring to instructors as "energizer bunnies" after my second visit to the studio because I sometimes saw things through the prism of television commercials. One day, I was talking about dance energy with Morgan, who worked at the front desk at the studio. She used the term too. Morgan was a team dancer for the Boston Celtics; she knew something about energy creation. Energy was one of the reasons Morgan, like so many students, was attracted to ballroom dancing. She, too, marveled at the capacity of instructors to work long hours, day after day. I had read that a well-trained athlete could create 300-400 watts of power, which is enough to run a television for several hours. On any given day, a dance instructor could easily match that.

There are pros and cons to being a student within a dance studio. In a large studio, there are many instructors with different skill levels and motivations. Melissa, my primary instructor, had always encouraged me to take both group and private lessons with other instructors to gain different perspectives. I joked with her and asked if instructing me had worn her out. But I took her advice and occasionally took private lessons, both within the studio and elsewhere. Melissa, understandably, would have preferred I take all my private lessons from other instructors within the studio. She could benefit from their observations, and the more lessons studio instructors taught, the better it was for the studio. My priority was to take lessons only from instructors who could best help me slay the dragon, regardless of where they worked. Dragon slayers were not that common within the instructor world and many students do not require one.

Early in my dance journey, I followed Lola's advice and tried to learn something from every dance instructor I met in a group class or on the dance floor. I had much to learn. Group lessons and social dancing were free at the studio, and things went well. My approach to a private lesson was different, because of life experience and the fact that there was a Dance Dragon in my head. Life experience had taught me it was better to listen to the advice of a few people who knew me well than a lot of people who hardly knew me. I was also skeptical about the motives and skill of people who offer advice or instruction for a fee. I needed, first, to become comfortable with their skill level and motivation, and to understand the parameters within which they worked. My hope with private lessons was that as the knowledge base between my instructor and myself grew, the pace of learning would increase. It was also why I wanted to understand dance from the instructor - or energizer bunny - perspective.

Instructor careers were full of risks. If the economy tanks, dance lessons can fast become a luxury students can't afford. The quantity, if not the quality, of dance instructors in most urban environments exceeds demand. If they become injured or sick, so their body isn't at 100 percent, their income and career advancement suffer. Long-term relationships between student and instructor are often complicated by studio priorities and agendas. The life circumstances of students change and dance can quickly be put on the backburner. Most importantly, instructors need to constantly add value for their committed students, not just newbies. Unlike "wedding people" and "fence-sitters," long term students spend considerable money on lessons. If they outgrow their instructor, or sense a lack of interest, they move on. The competing pressures to find and keep dance students, make money, grow, and be a good teacher all influence the behavior of energizer bunnies. When instructors cannot generate enough fees from existing students or develop new ones, some will poach students from other instructors.

One Saturday night, Eileen and I joined a few friends from our studio at a ballroom dance event in Newton, Massachusetts, held in a high-school auditorium. When we arrived that night, we paid our $15 and joined the group Argentine tango lesson. There were about 60 people in the class, evenly split between male and female. We found our friends but, for the most part, we were among strangers. The event consisted of an hour-long lesson by an experienced instructor followed by three hours of ballroom. Coffee, cookies, and something that resembled pizza had been placed on a few tables. The dance crowd that evening skewed older than most.

Eileen and I were more familiar with the American tango than the Argentine version. While there are variations of the Argentine tango the one we were doing involved considerable body contact. People were trying to dance chest-to-chest, and there was considerable thigh, knee, and lower body contact. The class was set up to rotate partners, and it soon became apparent that many dance partners were not comfortable with the body movement and physical contact. The Argentine tango may have been an odd way to introduce ourselves to this group, but we survived and had more than a few laughs in the process.

After the group lesson, the dance party began. I soon felt as if I was wearing an orange jacket during deer-hunting season. Whenever I was not dancing, a woman would ask me to dance. There were some good male dancers on the floor, so I knew my dance skill was not the primary reason for my attraction. Other than our friends from the studio, no one there had ever met me. At first, I was curious about my popularity.

Ann introduced herself. She was an attractive woman in a blue dress and asked me if I would like to do a foxtrot. In the spirit of ballroom dancing, I said yes. We chatted, and Ann quickly ascertained how long I had been dancing and where and what my preferences were, and extended the obligatory but often exaggerated compliments about my dancing. Eventually, I had a chance to deflect the focus from me and asked Ann her reason for attending. Ann told me she had always loved ballroom and had decided in her twenties to become an instructor. After a few years working in a studio, Ann determined she could better serve her students if she operated as an independent and focus 100% of her attention on the needs of her students rather than being a studio owner. Ann mentioned the accomplishments of her students, two of whom had once attended my studio. She let me know how long they had taken lessons, how convenient they found taking lessons with her at her home and that they would be willing to answer any questions I might have. The music for the foxtrot was still playing. We had talked through her entire sales pitch in less than three minutes.

As the night progressed, I danced with three more independent instructors. My answers became briefer as my skill at identifying instructors on the hunt evolved. Later, two instructors circled back to our table, offered me a free lesson, and left me their card. On the way home, Eileen asked me about my female partners that night. I answered that they were pleasant and mostly laid back. Eileen told me that she found some of the men chauvinistic and in need of a hygiene coach. Unlike me, Eileen had not been targeted by any instructors.

Upstairs at Ryles Jazz Club in Cambridge on Saturday nights, there is ballroom dancing, but it is quite different from the crowd at the high school auditorium in Newton. There is a bar and a DJ, and a crowd of 50 to 75 people. The space can be tight and as the night progresses it gets hot. Dancing starts at 10:00 p. m. and continues until 2 a. m. Ryles has an arrangement with a local dance studio, which allowed an instructor to offer a practice lesson, play DJ, and bring a few colleagues to prospect the crowd.

The instructors at Ryles are competent at both dancing and positioning their local independent studio as a hot studio in greater Boston, which it is. Most people who went to Ryles are either good social dancers or beginner students trying to improve. It was always a fun evening, and we sometimes stayed there into the early-morning hours. The energy level at Ryles was usually high, as was the noise level. If you met a dance instructor during a dance, conversation was tough so they focused on getting your email or phone number.

Fortunately, I learned early on that instructor-student courting and poaching were a necessary part of the ballroom scene. Most students, once they understand how often economics drives instructor behavior, become adept at managing the situation. If you want to play the game, you can get a free sample lesson before you commit. If you want to avoid the game, most instructors will back off from the hunt once you let it be known you have an existing relationship. Aside from frequenting group lessons and dance parties at studios or going to a club, the best way to meet other instructors is to ask students who know you well.

"I would be happy to have you lead me in a waltz," Neil announced. I looked at the faces of the eleven couples waiting for me to answer and thought about Neil's offer for about five long seconds. It meant that I would lead Neil, a male instructor, playing the role of follower, in a waltz in front of hundreds of people. The good news was that it would not be a solo performance; there would be 24 people on the dance floor. The bad news was Neil was the best dancer in the building and no one, except the people looking at me, would know why I was leading a male. Our performance dance was a synchronized waltz and all 12 couples had to move on the floor together. I lied to Neil and told him I would enjoy leading him in the waltz. No one else was available who knew the routine, and I could not say no to my class. My response caught the attention of the Dance Dragon. I could smell him.

Every summer you can find Neil Duncan at Ballroom Dance Camp (BDC), a five-day summer dance school in Rhode Island. A student at our studio had strongly recommended that Eileen and I attend the program. We had signed up for Neil's level-two classes with eleven other couples. It was a learning experiment. We had decided to test our capacity to learn together as a couple and have fun. For the first few days, Neil led his class of 12 couples through 6 separate hour-long lessons on different ballroom dances. We also worked for two hours each day on the group waltz performance.

By mid-week, my back was stiff and my mind was cluttered with dance steps and body moves. I kept focused on Neil, who was always dressed in black, standing in the middle of the room. I tried to absorb every word he said as well as some of the energy and positive thinking he brought to the class. The couples around us came from all over America. For some, this was their summer vacation. A person who dances for five consecutive days is eccentric, so I considered everyone at the camp as either a "committed one" or a "mad one. " It was tough for Eileen and me to keep up; I was slower, and when Eileen tried to help, it did not always work. Leaders have different roles than followers, and, like most good female dancers, Eileen had been trained to teach males.

I felt myself growing tense. There were moments when I was energized by a small accomplishment or the supportive words of a fellow dancer. But I knew I was on the road to mental and physical exhaustion; it was simply a question of when I would need to sit out a session. By Tuesday afternoon, I noticed we were not the only couple struggling to keep up.

Neil read the growing tension in the class well that day. He started walking among the dancers and dealing with us couple-by-couple. Dancing with the same person day after day for hours is a different experience than dancing in a group class with strangers and friends for a two-minute dance. Neil listened to various couples, never took sides in the often-heated disputes. and did some coaching. At times, he asked the more experienced couples to look around and help the less experienced. He worked hard at building an environment of inclusiveness. As the afternoon progressed, dancers appeared less inhibited about their shortcomings, the number of questions increased and Neil's energy transfusion seemed to give a boost to everyone. Later that evening, I asked Neil about his approach to teaching dance instruction. Neil was an energizer bunny; his face was still fresh after 12 hours of work, his eyes clear. Only his raspy voice hinted that he might be tired.

In this group class, Neil said he wanted dancers to experiment with a broad range of subject matter. He did not expect me or anyone else to master the content. What he hoped was that it would fuel us to learn over time. Neil saw camp as a laboratory where the student can try different things at his or her own pace and figure out what works best. We all learn in different ways. He suggested that after camp I talk to Eileen about what we'd learned and how we could practice.

Our camp class had committed to perform a synchronized waltz on Thursday night at the formal party. Eileen and I "volunteered" for the chance to perform. The fact was, the pressure to perform with your group was considerable. I was in a class too advanced for me. Neil had choreographed a dance that had couples crisscrossing the floor at a lively pace. If one couple was off beat, the chance of a collision would increase.

As the couple leader, our speed and direction were my responsibility.

Eileen was not happy with our last couples' practice that Thursday afternoon. She diagnosed my problem as a lack of effort and focus while I saw it more as a lack of comprehension of the choreography, and my skill level. I needed more time to practice, but that was not going to happen. Mostly, we were tired and needed an attitude adjustment. Dancing is supposed to be fun, and we were taking it too seriously. Whatever the source of the problem, there was serious tension between the two of us that Thursday. Early that evening, I was dressed in my tux, ready to go. I wanted to go for a walk around the hotel and relax on my own. I told Eileen I would meet her downstairs, and she said she'd join me in 20 minutes.

As I got off the elevator, I noticed that everyone in my class was gathered outside the ballroom in the pre-arranged line. It looked to me as if they were ready to go into the ballroom and perform. Nan and Tom, the couple next to us in the formation, saw me and asked where Eileen was. They said the performance would start in two minutes. I replied that we thought the dance was scheduled an hour from then. A note had been left on our dinner table, but we'd missed it. I felt the tension in my stomach. We had let the entire class down. I tried to reach Eileen on the cell but no luck. Anyhow, it was too late. I found Neil and told him we would not be in the line. "Dan, if you are not in the line, then it impacts everyone else's place on the floor," Neil said. He then asked me to dance with him.

I hadn't thought about the consequences of our absence in a group performance. I looked at Neil and reminded myself that trusting your partner, male or female, is a big part of dance. I had worked hard for five days and was satisfied with my effort, if not the result. I did not want to make a fool of myself on the dance floor, but the alternative was to let the group down. Neil looked at me, sensing the source of my hesitation, and waited for me to say yes. I told myself the Dance Dragon was not going to screw this up. One minute later, Neil and I walked side by side onto the ballroom floor with smiles on our faces. Only Neil's smile was real. We were about the same height, but as the only male couple we stood out. We took our position on the dance floor, the crowd cheered, and the waltz began. The dance itself was a blur. I didn't think about the crowd. I was focused on leading my male partner - someone with whom I had never danced - listening to the music, and remembering my steps. Neil followed my lead. Of course, there were times when I hesitated and Neil led me through a back step or two until I got back on track.

When the dance ended, everyone celebrated. Eileen arrived with a "what just happened?" look on her face. It was hard to say whether she was more shocked or embarrassed. The other dancers in our class were supportive and told her everything had worked out. Several people in the class asked Neil if the group could perform the routine again later in the evening with Eileen as my partner. Neil spoke to the organizers, and they agreed to a repeat performance. An hour later, I led Eileen onto the floor and the waltz began. I kept my frame and concentrated on the music. It was not my best dance of the evening, but I was relaxed and Eileen did a great job. After the performance, we enjoyed ourselves dancing to the sounds of a live band for several hours. The tension had passed.

On Friday morning, we said our goodbyes. Eileen and I had tested our dance stamina as well as our ability to learn as a couple despite the skill gap that existed between us. No doubt we would adjust our expectations the next time. I said goodbye to Neil and thanked him for being my dance partner. Ironically, dancing with Neil was an important lesson in my dance life. Whatever fear or self-doubt I had before I walked out onto the floor with him as my partner had been defeated. Now when I got frustrated, I would remember that dance. Neil was an energizer bunny and, I suspected, a dragon-slayer as well.

Chapter Thirteen

The Urge

I paid no attention to the few people in the airport terminal that evening. It was late and my earphones were plugged in. My son's plane had not yet arrived, and I had been sitting and listening to *Shackles*, a gospel song by Mary Mary that I played to hear the beat for the cha-cha. A powerful urge came over me, and I rose from my chair and walked to an open space maybe 20 feet away. I started to dance the cha-cha basic, digging my feet into the carpet, bending my knees and staying on beat. A year earlier, if I saw myself or anyone else dancing alone in an airport terminal I would have labeled them as eccentric.

While I was focused on the music and the dance, something weird happened, I drifted into a sort of trance. I found myself on a white cloud dancing with an unknown partner. I felt great. I was smiling and my entire body seemed to float with the music. When the song ended, I stopped dancing, snapped out of my trance and was back in the terminal.

Shackles was my favorite song for cha-cha practice because I could easily find the beat, and I never tired of the music. The song reminded me of gospel music I had heard in movies, and in person at several funerals. The urge to move my entire body in dance, not just my feet, was a phenomenon I was starting to feel, but could not explain. No doubt my interpretation of the opening lyrics "take the shackles off my feet so I can dance" was different than the songwriters originally intended. My shackles were all the negative thoughts the Dance Dragon conjured up in my mind. The Dance Dragon represented all the reasons why I suppressed my urge to dance as a youth. The song was liberating and reminded me of the early days of rock and roll with musicians like

Sam Cooke and the dancing I had watched but never did in my youth. At the airport that night I realized how much I had changed since the days of Elvis and Sam Cooke.

Rock and roll and television arrived together in America and impacted not only our media, music, and dance but also the way we interacted socially with each other. When Elvis appeared on the Ed Sullivan show, I was one of the sixty million people who watched him sing *Love Me Tender.* The television audience rating that night would be comparable to a Super Bowl game today. I did not care about television ratings then; I cared about my friends and how my peers would react to Elvis.

Elvis changed America, and most importantly, America's youth, in ways no one could ever imagine. The day after Elvis appeared, my sixth-grade male classmates were excited. We whispered among ourselves, so the nuns could not hear, about Elvis's long hair, his sideburns, and how he walked into a room. At the time, most institutions and parents where we lived required boys to keep their hair short. As for the girls in my class, they were years ahead of me. They liked Elvis's good looks and voice, but it was the way he moved his body that made them crazy. Their eyes were always laser-focused on his gyrating hips. At recess in the schoolyard, out of sight of the nuns, I would watch girls imitate the sighing, groaning and swooning that Elvis's body moves inspired. No mainstream white musician or dancer ever moved his lower body like Elvis. Some people within the religious establishment saw sin and sex in Elvis's hip moves and wanted him banned from the airwaves. Young girls saw something else. The networks tried to keep the critics happy by having the camera focus only on Elvis's upper body but that was not good for television ratings and was soon abandoned.

Most adults thought Elvis was a fad. Dick Clark perceived things differently. He saw rock and roll as a music and dance game-changer and television as the medium to make it happen. *American Bandstand* exposed a generation of young people to a combination of body moves and physical closeness that created not only a dance and music revolution but also a social revolution. From their homes, teenagers witnessed white youths dance to the music of black musicians like

Smokey Robinson, James Brown, and Aretha Franklin, and their own urge to dance overwhelmed them. In time, blacks would join white youth on the *Bandstand* dance floor. With racial mixing, the show became so controversial some local stations dropped it. Both television and rock and roll, however, were too powerful to be stopped, by those who saw either sin in dance, or the mixing of the races, as a threat to our society. By the sixties, Beatlemania had arrived and the social landscape of America was changed forever.

I loved the music of the 50's and 60's as well as the social revolution in the lyrics of Dylan, Baez, and the Beatles, but I resisted dance. I watched others dance from the sidelines. By the 70's, when I began my professional career in advertising, during the waning days of the era portrayed in *Mad Men,* I started to grasp the true impact television, music, and dance had on my generation. Young people wanted a lifestyle that was more honest and explicit about the opposite sex, physical appearance, and immediate gratification.

People had also become more open to everyday discussions with their peers about their appearance. They talked about the pimples on their face, the clothes they wore, their hair, and the smell of their breath and bodies. The use of breath mints and gum, deodorant, pimple-fighting creams, and scented shampoos exploded. A good-smelling body, tight jeans, and a smile with a full set of white teeth could dramatically improve a young person's popularity with the opposite sex, or at least that is what we in the advertising business promised. The focus on hygiene, cosmetics, and more provocative clothing bred new habits that impacted the way people presented themselves in our schools and work places, as well as on the dance floor.

Physical closeness and sensual body movement became more acceptable not only on the dance floor but in everyday situations depicted on television and in the movies. Viewership of dance shows like *American Bandstand* and *Soul Train* grew dramatically and ad revenue soared. Ironically, in my advertising life, I found myself making a living by promoting the benefits of a good-smelling body. I managed the Arrid antiperspirant account at a large New York advertising agency and advocated that my client allocate $10 million dollars a year for television ads. I reluctantly became an expert on preventing body odor and wet armpits. In our commercials, we used models in romantic situations to demonstrate how Arrid could help prevent body odor and reduce unsightly wetness. If you used Arrid every day, we implied, you could approach individuals of the opposite sex with confidence. We used attractive sexy women, like Elke Sommer, in the commercials to get attention and promote the brand promise "Get a little closer with Arrid Extra Dry." The visual presentation of closeness in our ads was as provocative as television allowed at the time.

Fast forward to today and television continues to be a powerful medium to promote whatever fantasies dancing might offer. The show *Dancing with the Stars* reaches 20 million viewers a week and inspires people of all ages and cultures to give ballroom dancing a try or, at least, watch attractive dancers dressed in provocative clothing and fantasize. The Internet with YouTube and 24/7 access to video has replaced television as the number-one medium and brings music and dancing of all types, not just to America, but to the entire world. Not only is YouTube a resource to jog people's memory about a dance step but it is a vehicle to enjoy great dance performances in both the past and the present. YouTube's impact on music and dance is the equivalent of television, radio, and the movies combined, on steroids.

I told myself that dancing to *Shackles* at the terminal was a good thing. My urge to dance spontaneously had increased. For the first time, I found myself in a public place totally absorbed in dance. Before, this had happened only at home or in another safe environment. And, when I surrendered myself to the music, I found myself drifting into a white cloud. I was not sure why this was happening. All I knew was that I wanted to spend more time on the white cloud. I needed to figure out how to make that happen.

One night, I was sharing a beer with my friend Kevin and explaining both the growing urge to dance and my desire to be on a cloud and truly feel the dance. Kevin was a social dancer, an active biker, and a yoga addict. He expressed a mixture of concern and fascination with my transformation from dance avoider to someone who wanted to dance on a white cloud. Kevin himself had loved to dance in his youth, but he was not sure he had ever traveled on a white cloud. As for the urge, our conversation confirmed I was clearly a very late bloomer.

Looking back now, I'm of the opinion that everyone is born with the urge to dance, but it needs to be cultivated when we are young or it will die. In my case, the desire to dance either died or was in a coma for several decades. I am not sure when or how it happened but I had resurrected the urge. Now I needed to feed and strengthen that desire if I wanted to become a better dancer. Kevin asked how often I felt the urge. I told him that my need to dance was not a 24/7 thing; I was not a "mad one", yet for me the desire arose within me most days. I described myself as moderately addicted. He smiled and said he was happy for me.

I was becoming desperate. I knew the frequency and intensity of my urge to dance depended on the people around me, the place I was in, the music and mood. If I was having a bad day at the office and wanted to change it to a good day, I thought of dance and closed my office door, taking a chance of being discovered. I went to Pandora and played music by Adele or Sam Smith or perhaps Pink Martini or the Gotan Project. I put my mind in the backseat, listened and turned the keys over to my body.

I needed to become smarter about increasing my own level of energy through exercise and what and when I ate before dancing. I stopped eating dinner before I went dancing. I tried drinking coconut water and eating fruit. Then I switched to eating a few handfuls of jellybeans or nuts and drinking smoothies. I dramatically increased my water intake. On Wednesday night after a group lesson and before the party, Cliff and I would often step out for tequila with lime juice. Some people believed that the agave plant from which tequila was derived has health benefits. Tequila helped me, but practically speaking I could only employ that tactic in the evenings and I needed to discipline myself to one drink or my sense of balance went askew.

I learned that we all have enormous amounts of potential energy stored in our bodies. Once humans are in motion, we start to create energy and that, in turn, creates real power. Movement causes oxygen and nutrients to interact with body tissue, gets our cardiovascular system moving, and stimulates our brain. The energy we create enables us to swim multiple laps, lift heavy snow, go for a five-mile run, or dance the night away. The challenge every day is to release our stored energy and create kinetic energy or the energy of motion.

I started to think more about the people around me on the dance floor and how their energy impacted me and kept me going. Energizer bunnies were always a good source, but the crowd on the dance floor was different. I have no idea, scientifically speaking, whether humans can transfer energy to each other, but, when dancing with certain people, I felt they could. One day, I asked Cliff if he thought dancing was addictive and where he got his energy.

"My medical friends tell me that body movement can produce endorphins, which are a form of opiate. They create a feeling of euphoria as well as inhibit the release of pain signals. In that sense, dancing is addictive just like running or skiing and that is not a bad thing. "

Cliff had been committed to the Paleo diet for years and was convinced it was part of the reason for his physical stamina. I had watched Cliff sometimes take four to five dance lessons a week and attend multiple dance parties. He never needed or perhaps never wanted to take a break. At his wedding, Cliff danced all night and did not stop until it was close to dawn. Like some other dance addicts, Cliff worked out most days with weights and took yoga lessons. Dancing, like running, may give people a natural high, but it also required that you provide your body with the energy and stamina to create that feeling and maintain it.

I started to study the people around me who on occasion displayed the urge, and noticed things I never saw before. When I heard music in a social setting, I'd scan the room for people who had that urge to move and was often surprised at who they were. I watched people with their headphones on the subway and sports fans at the ballpark. At weddings, I tried to predict who would end up on the dance floor and who would avoid it, as I once did. I observed children with their musical toys. I watched how they moved their bodies and clapped their hands when an adult led them. There was no battle between their body and mind; they were free. I wanted to join them.

My effort to increase my energy led me to a book called *Conditioning for Dance* by Eric Franklin. The author writes about muscles and how you can train your body through "self-talk" to relax and grow stronger, more flexible and energetic. The essence of Franklin's message was that we all tighten our muscles when we are tense or fearful. I learned that by doing this, I was using more energy and feeding the Dance Dragon. In sports or dance, if we tighten our muscles, muscle coordination, strength, and balance become more difficult. Tension consumes energy at an accelerated rate and wears us down.

I needed to find better ways to ignore mental stress or tension. Franklin recommended the best way to accomplish this was to conjure up positive images of ourselves in our mind. I concluded that daydreaming about myself dancing before actually dancing was a good thing. When I was a kid, I daydreamed about playing for the Boston Red Sox. As I walked to the Little League field, I conjured positive expectations of myself. I hit home runs, stole bases, and made great plays in the field. I guess back then that was my own version of self-talk. I have no idea whether self-talk helped my performance in Little League, but I don't remember feeling tense often when I played baseball.

I tried increasing my daydreams about dance. One hot August Sunday on a way to a dance studio, I stopped for gas at a rare full-service gas station in Roslindale, a neighborhood in Boston. As the attendant was pumping the gas, my window was down, and I was tapping my fingers on the side of the car. I was moving my head as I listened to Robert Palmer's *Addicted to Love,* and practicing "self-talk. " In my daydream, I saw myself smiling, doing a triple swing at a dance party. I was wearing a white panama hat, a purple crew-neck cotton t-shirt, black slacks, purple socks, and black-and-white dance shoes. My partner was dressed in a black-and-white polka-dot dress. I was relaxed, light on my feet with a full tank of energy. I was in my own world having a great time. A few minutes must have passed. The attendant came back with my credit card, looked at me to see if I had returned to earth, and said with a mostly toothless smile, "You like the beat, huh?" I smiled back and said yes. As I started to drive away, Eileen looked at me, and we both laughed.

I felt less mental stress practicing by myself than dancing with a partner or instructor. I moved my body better. I would often tell Melissa that I did my best dancing when I was alone. Of course, that was my opinion. My standards of a good practice session were a bit slack compared to those of Melissa. She worked hard in our lessons on body movement and self-expression. She was trying to get me to let go, relax, and minimize the stress I created on myself. Sometimes she succeeded, but there were times when my mind would not allow my body to cooperate anymore and we switched to dancing for fun. On occasion, the self-induced stress wore me down and, by the end of a lesson, my head and shoulders would be tilted forward. Franklin's book and Melissa's coaching helped me understand both my body and my mindset. I worked harder at experimenting with positive dance thoughts. If that failed and my posture became banana-shaped, then I resorted to remembering the image of Melissa imitating my poor dance posture.

One afternoon, after a lesson, Melissa came into the shoe room. She had my 8½ by 11 dance-lesson book held in her folded arms. The book was a record of every lesson I had taken. It was thick with paper and contained her notes on lesson recaps and suggestions for practice. Her face had a now-familiar look. I prepared myself for a conversation; the cynical side of me called it a sales pitch. Melissa would lead by throwing me a compliment. I would answer with a thank you or a question. She would then make suggestions about possible next steps in my dance education. It was part of the student-instructor conversational dance we did. Melissa liked to make big suggestions and then backtrack only if necessary. Melissa complimented me that day on my progress with body movement and self-expression and told me I was a different person on the dance floor than the first time I walked into the studio. I mentioned that when I first arrived I did not have the urge to dance. Now, not only did I want to dance, but my goal was to be better, stronger, and more confident in my dance. I wanted to get to a point where I felt my entire body was free and I could surrender to the music.

Dancing reminded me of skiing. Some days I would struggle with cold winds, dark skies, icy surfaces, and crowds on the slopes. I could not find my rhythm. Other days were sunny with blue skies and cool, crisp air. I could see for miles and the slopes were empty. I could find my rhythm and felt free to move across the snow. Skiing was pure joy. My urge to ski required that I be ready physically, mentally, and emotionally to experience those days. I told Melissa that I wanted to be ready whenever I felt the urge to dance.

Melissa listened and understood. She continued with her well-practiced pitch. There was an event coming at year-end in Washington D. C called Dance-O-Rama. She thought it would accelerate my learning and confidence. She made no promises about the white cloud other than to help make it happen for me. The event lasted three days, and there was competition in six different dance categories. She suggested I challenge myself to do a solo with her in this major venue. "We could do a rumba."

Whenever Melissa exceeded my expectations with her suggestions, I usually responded by shaking my head sideways, exhaling, and returning her smile. She would then give me a quizzical look and say "What?" as if she was surprised that I was surprised. Like a dance, our conversation had a pattern to it and we took turns leading. We had heard each other's thoughts and I hit the pause mode by saying "I need to think it over." Melissa agreed. She knew I liked to think things out. In this case, we both knew she would be back on the offensive in a few weeks.

Chapter Fourteen

The Land of Dance

My mind was fixated on pursuing the feel of the dance. I wanted to know how to find the white cloud and float with the music. When I started dancing, I was curious about the rumba, cha-cha, and mambo. I thought Latin dances required more energy and passion than the foxtrot and waltz. As a young adult, I lived in New York City and worked and socialized with Cuban Americans. I traveled to Puerto Rico frequently on business. My client in Puerto Rico was born in Cuba and insisted that when I came to San Juan we go out at night to local Cuban-style dance clubs. When he came to New York, he wanted to experience the Cuban dance nightlife as well. He loved to dance and I was happy to watch, enjoy my beer, and absorb the Latin club atmosphere.

At the studio, Elena introduced me to Cuban motion movement in a cha-cha group class. I watched her slowly bend one knee forward and drive her foot down into the floor while she straightened the opposite leg. Elena would then repeat the motion with her other knee. Her hips and butt moved as if her body were controlled by the music. Her dancing might be called sexy by dancers, though perhaps sexually offensive by those who saw dance as sinful. Elena also demonstrated that simply wiggling your bum side to side to the beat of the music was not Cuban motion. As a man with a small bum and no serious wiggling experience, that was good news. The bad news was most American-Anglo men didn't grow up knowing how to put a sway in their hips. For a beginner dancer, hip-sway took considerable practice to learn. The knees became the focal point of your dance and your hips followed their lead. I needed to feel the rhythm of Cuban motion in my body and then let the music take over. I struggled with that feeling, as it was different from anything I had ever done. My dance buddy Lola told me many times about the need to feel the music first and only then to let go. I understood the concept, but I struggled to learn it.

Several days after my group lesson with Elena, Eileen gave me a photo journal book called *Dance in Cuba* by Gil Garcetti. The photographer had spent thirty-two years working in the Los Angeles County District Attorney's office, for the last eight of which he was the elected District Attorney. Garcetti's professional career as a prosecutor no doubt exposed him to the many faces and emotions of humanity. When he went to Cuba, his photographer's eye captured the raw and powerful emotions Cubans expressed in dance. Garcetti put on film what Kapka Kassabova and Catalina Midori captured with words in their novels on the tango and the mambo. The photographs of Cuban dancers, with their mixture of African and European blood and their history of poverty and struggle, gave dance, in my eyes, an earthy and honest face that I had not often seen in American ballroom dance studios. In Garcetti's photographs, I saw dance as the antidote Cubans used to offset their poverty, communicate with each other, and celebrate life.

A few months later, while Eileen and I were visiting friends in Maine, the idea of traveling to Cuba surfaced. My friends had been asking me questions about my dance lessons, and I'd said I wanted to see people who gave themselves up to the music without any frills or pretense. In my opinion Cuba was such a place. Our friend Carroll's father had lived in Havana; Cindy liked the idea of acquiring a first-hand insight into Cuban culture, and Tom and Hank talked about the legacy of Ernest Hemingway, smoking Cuban cigars, and drinking Cuban rum. Consensus was quickly reached among the six of us. The tipping point was the fact that a friend in Boston owned a travel company that ran tours to Cuba through the People to People government program. At the time, the U. S. -sanctioned program allowed small groups to travel to Cuba legally on education or cultural tours. My friend knew the island well. I talked to him about dance and music, and it did not take long before we signed up for the trip.

Cuba was one of the most unusual places on earth. The Cuban people lived for the last 50 years under a U. S. embargo in what had been labeled, until 2015, a "terrorist" country by the U. S. government. Its location, 90 miles off the coast of Florida, climate, and history, along with its reputation for great cigars, music, and dance, all contributed to the Cuban mystique. Cuba's global reputation for music and dance received a boost in the 1990s when the Buena Vista Social Club recording was released. The album was named after a club in Havana where famous Cuban musicians gathered in the 1940s. Some of the musicians in the recording had played at the club 50 years earlier. The musicians were invited to play in Europe and at Carnegie Hall in New York City, and their performance resulted in a documentary that was nominated for an Academy Award.

Our trip to Cuba exposed us to a small rural elementary school as well as the National Art School in Havana, tobacco farmers and fishermen, dancers and musicians. The six of us landed at Cuba's Jose Marti Airport, near Havana, where we were joined by a couple from the Midwest and two women from the West Coast. Additionally, a representative from the tour company, as well as a Cuban government tour guide, traveled with us for nine days. Both men knew Cuba well.

The first sign that we had arrived in a land like no other was the airport parking lot. Cars and vans of a recent vintage from China, Eastern Europe and Russia were mixed with American-made Chevrolets and Fords in bright colors from the 1950s. The juxtaposition of the influence of America culture in Cuba in the 1950s, Russian culture from the 1960s through the 1990s, and now to some degree Chinese culture was a theme we would see played out throughout our stay. The other cultural theme, and more central to our visit, was the blend of Spanish and African influences that had evolved over the centuries, and today made Cuban art, music, dance, and religion unique.

On our way to lunch, our group drove through the colonial heart of the city. As we passed decaying buildings, I noticed the smiling faces of healthy-looking people on the street. The contrast with many urban poor areas of America was clear. The people walked with their heads up and carried themselves with a sense of pride. When we reached the harbor, we saw several preserved colonial-era mansions, churches, parks, and the former fortress, protecting the huge harbor. Tourist books correctly describe this part of Havana as one of the most beautiful colonial-era cities in the world. At lunch, I sipped a welcome drink of rum and soda at a café while looking out on the water, absorbing the ocean breeze and sun. The first thing I noticed was how handsome the people walking along the sea wall were. The second thing was the live music in the small park adjacent to the cafe and how everyone in the vicinity seemed to move their body to the beat.

After lunch, we took a walk on the Malecón, a five-mile-long promenade around Havana's harbor, which was a world-class people-watching site. I watched my friend Tom stop at the sea wall and unconsciously start to move his body to the music playing nearby. A young schoolgirl, walking with friends, saw Tom moving his body to the music, came right up next to him, and started to move her body to the music with him. For this young girl, it was simply a spontaneous reaction to music. For Tom, it was something that never happened in Maine.

To help us better understand the Cuban people and the importance of music and dance in their lives today, we spent the morning of our second day with Alberto Faya, an expert on the history of Cuban music. As he told it, the Spanish "discovered" Cuba in the fifteenth century and proceeded to eliminate the indigenous population. By the late sixteenth century, music on the island was, for the most part, European. As more and more African slaves were brought to the island to farm sugar cane and tobacco, however, the music went through a slow process of Africanization. Slaves were required to speak Spanish and to practice Catholicism, but their souls and their music and dance remained African.

Since the various African tribes did not share a common language, music and dance served as a major means of communication. By the 18th century, through religion and other cultural interactions, the lines between Spanish and African music were also effectively blurred. This process planted the seeds for what is Cuban music today. Catholicism, the religion the slaves were forced to practice, evolved into the popular Santeria religion. We attended a Santeria ceremony in Havana and witnessed people worshiping through dance. I had spent 16 years in

Catholic schools and the mixture of West African animal sacrifice and voodoo drumming that accompanied the dance and body movement during the ceremony was beyond anything I had experienced in my religious education.

Alberto demonstrated how the musical elements of the Spanish guitar mixed with the percussion instruments and rhythm of African music permeated every aspect of the island's culture. Faya introduced us to the clave, the conga drum and the bongo bell. He explained that in Afro-Cuban music the five-stroke clave pattern was the structural core that held the rhythm together in dances such as the rumba, salsa, mambo, and cha-cha. It was this pattern that Alberto said activated the strong urge to dance among the Cuban people. This same pattern, influenced by African slaves, could be found in other Caribbean, South and North American music, including the samba and American jazz and swing. Alberto had spent his life studying music, and his discussion of how certain instruments and patterns could create an urge to dance helped me better understand music and myself.

That afternoon, we met with the Cuban Minister of Culture who explained to us that music, dance, and baseball, in that order, are the most important influences on Cuban culture today. They are the core activities around which people socialize. Unlike the United States, where slavery was concentrated in the South and linked to cotton farming and tobacco, in Cuba, African slaves were the majority population in the country by the end of the eighteenth century. When slavery ended in 1886, most Cubans had no education, a short life-expectancy, and few possessions. Today the Cuban people are well-educated and have a long life-expectancy, but poverty is still everywhere. Smart phones, fast-food restaurants, social media, and televised sports are not part of everyday life. Cubans primarily listen to music, dance, and play or watch baseball. It helps explain why they excel at all three activities.

The words of the Cuban Minister of Culture helped me understand why Cuba was so alive with the feel of the dance. They also made me realize the similarities and differences in the histories of our two countries and how that impacted our music and dance. Cuba, a poor communist country with a population of ten million, was a former colony of Spain and most of the population traced their roots to Africa and slavery. America, the wealthiest country on earth, with more than 300 million citizens, is a country whose population is descended primarily from European immigrants and, more recently, immigrants from Latin America and Asia. People, for the most part, came to our country by choice and enjoyed a level of personal freedom and expression that has never existed in Cuba. Of course, slavery and poverty are a part of American history too and clearly impacted our music and dance. Jazz music and swing dancing are but two testaments to that fact and, in time, they would mingle with the sounds and music of Cuba. Dance historians often pinpoint the European waltz in the early 19th century as the beginning of ballroom, and the Afro-Cuban influence, more than a century later, for dramatically broadening ballroom's appeal. What is important to understand is that the music and dance of ballroom as we know it today were not initially accepted by society.

In Europe, the waltz was met with tremendous resistance by English high society. English aristocrats saw the waltz as a German peasant dance. In America, where social class was less of an issue than in Europe, religious and racial biases impeded the acceptance of the waltz, swing, and other dances. In his book *Modern Dances*, the Rt. Rev. Mgr. Don Luigi Satori, an American Catholic priest, told Catholics that dancing the waltz was equivalent to committing adultery. An excerpt from the book provides a context for his rejection. "Consider the immodest pose taken in the waltz, and if you are not already blinded by lust, you will admit that it [the waltz] is in direct violation of the Sixth Commandment. " The immodest pose that the Monsignor was referring to in the waltz is what's known in dance as the "closed position", in which a man and a woman hold each other's hands, face each other, and dance in each other's arms. If the Monsignor was right about the waltz being a violation of the sixth commandment, hell will be full of ballroom dancers.

In the 1920s, seventy years after slavery legally ended in the United States, segregation kept blacks and whites from dancing the swing on the same floor. Black musicians such as Louis Armstrong and Billie Holiday changed the way white Americans experienced music and dance and helped evolve the American ballroom dancing scene. More recently, the growing popularity of Latino music and dance and the appeal of artists such as Jennifer Lopez, Ricky Martin, and Shakira have had a similar impact. The voices, rhythms and body movements of black and Latino musicians, many of them influenced by the same Afro-Cuban music I heard in Cuba, would urge a generation of white people onto the dance floor and encourage them to move their bodies in ways they had never imagined.

Chapter Fifteen

The Feel of Dance

On the third day of our trip, I found myself in the mountains of Western Cuba, listening to the rhythms of Cuban music and experiencing the urge to dance that Alberto Faya had mentioned. We had traveled to Vinales, about 125 miles southwest of Havana. Our destination was a 26-room hotel in a rural village called Las Terrazas, located in a biosphere reserve. We were escaping from the typical tourist path. The area is a mix of pine and tropical forests, rivers, waterfalls, and hills. The self-contained community of 1,000 or so is responsible for maintaining the area and promoting and supporting an eco-tourism industry. In addition to the farmers, a disproportionate number of the population made their living as crafts people, artists, and mountain guides. Rural Cuba portrayed a lifestyle that had been in existence for hundreds of years in which the people lived off the land, worked with their hands, enjoyed all that nature had to offer, and knew the feel of the dance.

The hotel was not fancy and we were the only Americans there. The plan was to visit artists, musicians, tobacco farmers, and an elementary school over three days. We ate most of our meals with local families. At night, we would sit on the patio, mix with the other guests, enjoy a Cuban beer and listen to a local band. The patio accommodated thirty to forty people, and there was space to dance. The weather conditions that first night were unusual for Cuba. We were in a forest with a wind chill of forty degrees Fahrenheit. In addition to our group of twelve, there were about a dozen German and English tourists, four Cuban band members, and several of their girlfriends, shivering on the patio.

All of us, including the bartender, were dressed in sweaters and windbreakers and wearing variations of sneakers and hiking shoes.

The bandleader, a young man named Ramon, was handsome, full of charm, and musically talented. Within half an hour, he convinced everyone to dance and several of us to play a musical instrument. I found myself, a man with no musical experience, playing the clave for a slow rumba dance song, with Ramon on one side and a tall German doctor playing the bongo drums on my other side. The doctor appeared to know what he was doing. I didn't. At first, I was uncomfortable playing with the band, but soon realized they were grateful for our presence that cold night. They were doing everything they could to keep us engaged.

After ten minutes, I was relieved of my clave responsibilities and returned to dancing ballroom rumba. I continued to watch the musicians play their instruments. The bongo drum and the clave played dominant roles in producing the sound of the beat, and I tried to listen and surrender to the sound. The energy and slow body movement of the young band was intoxicating and dancing the basic rumba for me became effortless and spontaneous. I was under the stars in the woods on a brisk night in a place far removed from the rest of the world. Nature, music, and the people around me, and nothing else, were on my mind. My body felt free to move. It was one of those moments that you could not plan. I was on the white cloud dancing to the music, and all my senses enjoyed what life had to offer. Cuba was made for music and dance, and I had just experienced the feel of the dance.

The next day, we went to a small elementary school that was probably comparable to a rural school in America 50 years ago. My daughter-in-law was raised in rural South Dakota and on occasion has told us about the one-room schoolhouse she attended. This Cuban schoolhouse had two classrooms with lots of old books and magazines held together with tape and staples. We were told art, music, and dance were a big part of the students' daily educational experience. There were no computers or televisions. There were, however, about 40 happy and beautiful children. their faces various shades of black and brown.

Outside, a group of children were playing volleyball and several of us were asked to join in. We communicated with our hands and eyes as we did not speak Spanish and the children did not speak English. I wondered what those children were thinking as they watched the gringo strangers. Later, we would listen to the school principal describe the educational system in Cuba. As he talked, parents arrived with lunch, which they ate with their children. Before we went on our way, Yelenda, a seven-year-old girl, asked to sing a song for us.

Yelenda was maybe four feet tall, her black hair cut short, and her big brown eyes dominated her face. Her smile included a few missing teeth, common for a child her age. She stood in front of the group and launched into a song about Cuba, and started to sway her body. Yelenda had no inhibitions. She sang and moved her body to reflect what she felt. Her voice and body movements sent a message of friendship to her gringo visitors that was clear and honest. With the high-pitched voice of a child, Yelenda clapped her hands, stomped her feet, bent her knees, and moved every part of her body to the sound of her own voice. Her classmates joined in and supported her with their clapping, swaying, and foot-stomping. Yelenda's voice never faltered as she kept eye contact with her audience. This seven-year-old girl from rural Cuba was not a trained performer; she was a messenger of friendship and used song, rhythm and body movement as her language.

After the young girl's performance, our group was asked in turn to sing a song. We were a group of ten gringos. We could not match the emotional impact of Yelanda's message, nor her talent, but we tried, and that was appreciated.

The next day, we visited the home of a seventh-generation tobacco farmer. We enjoyed Cuban coffee and cake with his family, toured his small farm, and smoked cigars. The farmer hand-rolled a cigar for each of his guests. While there was a time in my life when cigars were a daily routine, and I enjoyed them immensely, I had smoked rarely in recent years. I felt obligated to accept his gift and proceeded to make myself dizzy. Fortunately, I escaped to the outdoors and slowly recovered. The simplicity of the farmer's life and his surroundings reminded me that Cubans live their daily life at a different pace than most Americans and are more focused on the moment.

We moved on through the mountains and stopped at a large roadside tent for a light lunch. We were seated at a long table while an all-female band played Cuban music outside on the grass in the drizzle. The lead singer had a strong smoky voice and the band seemed oblivious to the weather. A Cuban family sitting at a table near us had gathered to celebrate a young woman's birthday. They were dressed for the occasion and their smiles and soft laughter caught our attention. A young man, either a boyfriend or husband, rose from the table and asked the woman to dance. The tall, thin woman, in a long green dress, was initially caught off guard and tried to resist but finally agreed with a smile. The man, dressed in a dark suit and open-collared shirt had the build of an athlete, happy eyes, and a million-dollar smile. The couple walked to an open area on the wet grass and danced to *Chan*, a song about a young woman and her male friend at a beach. They were oblivious to the light rain and never took their eyes off one another as they danced effortlessly, as one. The feeling of love they exchanged during their dance was not a performance it was the real thing. When the music ended, they returned to the table as if the dance that they had just completed was nothing out of the ordinary. "Wow," I quietly said to myself.

When we arrived back at the hotel, the temperature was in the fifties and the rain had stopped. It was still cold by Cuban standards, but fine for us. We went to the outdoor bar and joined the band members and several of their young female friends. Ramon, the one member of the band who could speak English, asked about our day. I talked to him about my desire to become a better dancer. He mentioned every Tuesday he ran a free all-day dance session in the village, and people of all ages and skill levels came. He invited us to come. For our group that would have been a great way to spend a day in Cuba but the terms of the People to People tour did not allow us to adjust our trip on the fly. We told Ramon we needed to leave in the morning and return to Havana. He committed to teach us a dance or two later that evening.

When the band started to play, we were beyond relaxed. The mountain air smelled fresh after the rain, the stars were out, and the people around us were happy. Life didn't get much better. Within an hour, the "crowd" that evening peaked at about thirty people. My mind was totally focused on the music when a young Cuban woman, Maria, who had introduced herself to us at the bar earlier in Spanish, rose from her chair and started to dance. Maria was wearing a small white tee shirt and jeans, had long straight black hair that flowed down her back, brown silky skin, and a flirtatious smile. She danced as if she were by herself, alone in the forest. Every part of her body, even the timing of her breathing moved in perfect harmony to the music. It was as if Maria was in a trance dancing for Cuba that night. This young lady danced simply for the joy of dancing, and she had both the physical and emotional capacity to do it well. I saw her dance as an expression of her freedom and her passion for life. That night she showed the feel of the dance for me.

My inability to stop watching Maria dance made me wonder if I was being rude. However, I looked around and realized that the eyes of every person on the patio were fixed on Maria. You would have to be dead not to watch her. I decided to take a picture with my iPhone. I realized in some cultures my act would be considered inappropriate but that when it came to dance in Cuba that would not be the case. As the evening went on, I occasionally glanced over at Maria as she sipped her beer and moved her body to the music. She was at peace with life.

My mind drifted to the band and I wondered what they thought of this random collection of Europeans and North Americans trying to dance. Ramon seems to have sensed the struggle some were having and suggested it was time for a lesson. He showed us a simple dance consisting of three side steps and then a hip movement. In ballroom dancing, it is called the bachata. The Cuban band members and their girlfriends, including Maria, demonstrated the dance several times. They seemed to be having fun. After ten minutes, most of us had the basic movement down and for the rest of the night we all did our best to move our bodies to the beat like our Cuban hosts. As I watched this mix of German, English, and Spanish-speaking people enjoy dance in the rural mountains of Cuba, I remembered a comment Lola had once made: "If everyone understood the joy of dance there would be no war."

I went to Cuba to understand why music and dance were so important to the Cuban people, but also to learn more about the urge to dance, so I could pursue the mystery of the feel of the dance. I never had a conversation with Yelenda, Maria, or the young couple at the mountain restaurant about moving their bodies to rhythm. I simply watched. Despite a language barrier, they had showed me what their own feel of the dance was with their eyes and the way they moved their bodies. Dance was not about their appearance, the clothes or shoes they wore, the dirt or cement they danced on or the steps they took. Dance was about music and movement, people and place, and how together they created a feeling of freedom within us, along with a desire to share that feeling with others. Dance was a wordless language used to express honest feelings of joy, love, friendship, togetherness, and passion.

Four days later, we left Cuba. I wanted to learn how to discover and express my own feelings in dance— not to copy another person's dance. On the plane to Miami, I listened to reggae music on my headphones. As I dozed in and out of sleep, the music brought back memories of my many long cab rides in heavy traffic between Manhattan and JFK airport, on my way to and from Puerto Rico. The cab drivers were mostly Dominican or Jamaican at the time, not Cuban, and they controlled the radio dial. The music of Bob Marley played often. Marley's song *Roots, Rock and Reggae* came up on my headphone. I listened again to the lyric "Feel like dancing, dance 'cause we are free." Now I know what Bob Marley meant when he sang about dancing. I wanted to feel free.

Chapter Sixteen

The Day the Urge Stopped

Monday, April 15, 2013, was a bad day in Boston. That day I had no urge to dance. Music, the people around me, and my mood simply could not make it happen. Two bombs exploded at the Boston Marathon finish line. Three people were killed; hundreds of people were injured, and sixteen lost legs. Over the course of that week, our studio dance community would learn that a young dance instructor at the studio, Adrianne Haslett, had been hurt. Adrianne had been blessed with long legs, brown eyes, and a strong voice. On Saturday mornings, Adrianne stood in front of a group of students for 45 minutes, turned the music up, and taught a rhythm class. There was a lot of energy and most of us never took our eyes off Adrianne as she led us through dance and rhythm drills. She was young, beautiful and doing what she loved. It was a great way to spend a Saturday morning.

The Sunday before the bombing, Eileen and I walked down Boylston Street. We smiled at the people taking pictures of their children, posing as runners at the finish line of the Boston Marathon. It was inconceivable that spring afternoon to imagine the scene that would be played out there the next day. Pictures of Boylston Street would dominate the world news for days. Many of us would personally know one or more people who were injured in that attack. All of us who lived in Boston would feel anger, sadness, resolve, and pride in our community in the days ahead.

Until you have personally tried to run a marathon, it is hard to understand how focused a runner is on crossing that finish line. Either you finished the race or you didn't. There was no other option. There were times during a marathon that my body had told my brain I had to stop. However, the crowd along the last few miles pushed me to keep going. For many runners, the crowd wins you over and, because of them, you find the will to continue. Among those cheering at that finish line that day were Adrianne and her husband Adam. He had just returned from a tour of duty in Afghanistan, serving in the U. S. Air Force.

As often happens at the beginning of a mind-altering event, I had trouble processing how the bombing impacted my own life and that of my family and friends. When I first heard the news, I wondered if people I knew were hurt, but realized it could take hours or days before I had the answer. Part of me said I had to be patient and keep doing what I planned to do. In our case, Monday nights were a big dance night for both Eileen and me. We often scheduled our weekly private lessons then, and stayed for several group lessons. We enjoyed the small group of regular dancers who attended the Monday group classes. That day, however, the more we thought about dancing, the more we realized for many reasons we could not do it. We called to cancel our lessons and learned that the studio, like most other organizations in Boston that day, had already made the decision to close. The reality of the situation and the sadness, pain, and anger were beginning to sink in.

On Tuesday, we received an email from the studio saying only that Adrianne had been seriously injured in the attack and was in the hospital. Based on a request by the family for privacy, no other details were provided. We didn't go to the studio that day; like many people in Boston, our daily routine seemed insignificant amid stories of the dead, injured and the remarkable people in law enforcement and emergency care who responded with courage, compassion, and leadership. The best antidote for evil is goodness, and there was plenty of it in the community of Boston after the bombing,

I had to go out for a run. The running scene in the movie *Forrest Gump* had always been one of my favorites. Forrest ran and ran until the pain was gone. Running had always been a great cure for whatever troubled me. I thought about the thousands of runners in the marathon and their families and friends searching to find them in all that confusion. I kept thinking of an eight-year-old boy named Martin who liked to play baseball. Martin had been killed at the finish line. I had been a Little League coach in Boston for ten years. Helping kids learn to play baseball was one of the best things I had done in my life. I wondered how his family and teammates would channel the pain of seeing Martin's life destroyed into something positive. I wondered about Adrianne and hoped for the best.

Wednesday came and my mood had not changed. I had no urge to dance. Ironically, it was the day I had scheduled to take my dance test and officially move on to the next level. I had arranged a 5:15 pm class with Melissa for a final practice, and then would do my test with Kristen, the studio head, at 6:00 pm. When I woke up that morning, the last thing I wanted to do that day was dance. I wanted to run and get lost in my work. Later in the day, I tried practicing some dance combinations, but quickly gave up. There was no positive energy in my body. I was still living in a deep fog.

The first person I saw when I arrived at the studio that night was Richie. He had been dealing with his own serious health problems. He'd been told he should stop dancing while he waited for some test results on his lungs. We talked about Adrianne and, while there was no new information, it was obvious how hard the instructors were working to stay positive. I tried to be energetic and outgoing as well, but acting happy when I'm sad is not something I do well.

I walked out onto the dance floor to warm up, to see if I could change my mood and find some energy. I wasn't successful. When Melissa arrived, I found myself initially avoiding eye contact. I had seen too many sad eyes on the streets of Boston that day. Melissa asked me if anyone I knew other than Adrianne had been seriously hurt. I told her no, but I was sad and angry and was having a very difficult time focusing on dancing in the moment. We looked at each other and realized it was going to take some effort to dance on both our parts. Melissa started the class with a firm resolve to get our minds completely into dancing for forty-five minutes. I had taken many lessons from her and, whatever baggage from the day I might bring to a class, she usually succeeded in getting my mind focused on dance. It would not happen that day. Occasionally, for a minute or two, I would execute what she was teaching, but then I quickly drifted back into the fog.

I was frustrated with myself for not being able to concentrate. I was making a young instructor work so hard while Adrianne was seriously injured in the hospital. Melissa was doing a great job of holding herself together, and I was not. Yet I was the one with all the life experience. Melissa took me through the school figure basics that I would be tested on after our lesson. I knew the steps but I could not get them right that day. We tried dancing to an upbeat foxtrot and then a swing, but I was a wet noodle. I apologized several times for my lack of focus. Melissa's therapy in this awful situation was dancing, but I was still trying to figure mine out.

When the class ended, I had a five-minute break before Kristen walked toward me to start the test. Sadness and stress blanketed her face. For two days, she'd balanced the responsibility of keeping the studio going while making sure every student was aware of Adrianne's general situation. Kristen would be the first to tell you that she was an emotional woman. Dance was a big part of her life, and she'd had her own injuries and knew what it is like not to be able to dance.

While we talked about the bombing, I fumbled through the school figures. Kristen needed to talk more than dance. We talked about how certain violent events could forever change our lives and that we would never forget them. The school shooting in Newtown, Connecticut; the World Trade Towers bombing of 9/11, and now the marathon bombing. We talked about the need to make good out of evil, but we were each lost as to what possible good could come of this. As I listened, I saw in Kristen a young woman who probably never imagined there would be a day like this in her life. I saw her resolve to carry on. Regardless of how she felt as an individual, Kristen was taking one day at a time. She had to run a business, lead her young instructors through the days ahead, deal with scores of students who were concerned and keep the studio running. There was no going back to normal. If dance was Melissa's therapy, then Kristen's was talking through things.

The third instructor present that afternoon was Rachel. I had known Rachel since the day I arrived at the studio, and we'd danced together at most parties. I'd also occasionally taken lessons from her. She was always happy to help me with my cha-cha. If there was a position at the studio called "Chief Happy Officer", Rachel would have the job. When my test with Kristen was finished, Rachel walked by and we just looked at each other, and she asked me if it would be okay if we hugged. We hugged. I watched Rachel do lots of hugging in the next few days. She was good at it, and it was good for all of us. I had no idea how well I did my dance steps during the test, but I passed. Kristen, as was the custom, made the announcement, and I received a few cheers from those who were in the ballroom but the energy was still lacking. Clearly the bombing had taken the joy of dancing from all of us.

I went to the water cooler and thought about all the positive emotional support that co-existed with the anger within the dance studio that day. I thought about how many homes, offices, small businesses, churches, and community gathering-places in Boston were participating in that same struggle. The bombing had impacted thousands of people, yet the pain of this tragedy was most intense at the level where it becomes personal. Adrianne was a member of our dance studio's community, and that made the bombing personal. The thought of her lying in a hospital with a serious injury because of a sick-minded terrorist was hard to understand or accept. Shock, grief, sadness, and pain filled the room, and the only way we could reduce it was to turn and support each other.

I was happy to see Eileen when she arrived. We decided to try to dance. We joined Fran, Eileen's instructor, and a few other people, in a group class. Everyone did their best to try to forget the troubles. Swing music can be energizing and Fran, who had arrived from Spain a year before, was a great teacher. Students loved his classes. We all tried to climb the hill of positive thinking and some made progress, but for most of us it was temporary. Collectively, our eyes could not conceal our true feelings. We could not find the energy. Neither the music, the energizer bunnies, or the dancers in the room could make it happen that day, When the class ended, Eileen and I looked at each other and wordlessly acknowledged that dancing tonight was too tough. We had to leave. As Eileen later explained in an email to the studio staff, "We just could not pretend to be happy when we were so sad. " She wrote that we would be there the next night, for the ninety-minute dance party, and do our best to convince others to do likewise. Somehow we had to get the positive energy switch back on.

Thursday, April 18th, was another long day in Boston. Sadness was giving way to more acts of kindness and support to each other. Energy was returning to our city. I could see it on the streets, in the subways and in the stores. There was patience and a collective determination to defeat evil with goodness. There was a confidence that the police and military would find the individuals responsible for the bombing, and there was universal support for the effort they were making. The scale of the manhunt going on around Boston reminded me of the movies, with helicopters, police, and soldiers everywhere.

Thursday night dance parties were the highlight of the week at the studio. All the instructors attended and made the effort to dance with everyone. Adrianne was no exception, and we usually danced once or twice at each party. Whenever I danced with an instructor, I tried to do my best. I put pressure on myself. Usually, it was counterproductive. I tried to pick up the nuances of the different instructors. With Adrianne, I would often catch her looking over her shoulder as I tried to lead her around the floor. I often said to myself that I should take a lesson from Adrianne someday. No doubt I could learn from her and she would learn that I did everything possible to avoid collisions.

As that Thursday night approached, I knew both Eileen and I would go to the dance studio with a different attitude. We would dance all night, and we would be supportive of the instructors and every student who showed up. We all needed to do our best, otherwise we were letting evil win. The studio was not crowded. People in their conversations did not ignore the reality of the bombing or the impact it had on all of us. We talked about it with our dance partners, we asked each other about our feelings and did our best to offer support. Music and dance started to work that night. In a quiet way, each of us discovered that evening what we suspected; Adrianne had lost her leg. Perhaps that kept us all dancing, as we knew how important dancing was to Adrianne's life.

Near the end of the evening, I found myself dancing with Melissa to Neil Diamond's *Sweet Caroline.* I mentioned to her the song that was being played in major-league ballparks across America that night in support of the people of Boston. Melissa, who, is not a baseball fan, asked why. I explained that *Sweet Caroline* was a feel-good song that brought the people of Boston together. Years ago, the song was played over the loud speaker at Fenway Park during the eighth-inning break. The fans started to sway back and forth and sing. In Boston, people sing *Sweet Caroline* sometimes as a form of celebration and at other times as a song of togetherness.

The studio was very much together that night. I could feel the emotion. Somehow the music, and the collective mood of the people in the room, came together and succeeded in turning the energy back on. We found our urge to dance, not to celebrate, but to come together and honor all those who'd been hurt. Eileen and I stayed until the last dance and then some. We smiled and chatted and, like other dancers, did our best to support the instructors. Melissa chatted up a storm about some music that I should listen to that would help me with the beat. I watched the designated chief hugger, Rachel, wish people good night. I also thought about how this small group of young dance instructors would feel after the last student walked out the door and their thoughts turned to Adrianne and the pain of her losing her leg.

The emotional ups and downs of the marathon bombing week were intense. I felt anger, sadness, togetherness, and support. Within the dance studio and across Boston, I was exposed to scores of the positive feelings that small acts of human kindness, prayer, smiles, touches, and hugs can generate. When I connected on the dance floor on Thursday night with members of the studio tribe with my eyes, my hands, and body movement, I realized the dark side of life had been defeated. People in Boston and elsewhere that week came together to express feelings of support and to honor the victims of violence. Some people expressed themselves in words. I had expressed my own feelings in dance.

Chapter Seventeen

Hemingway's Men, A Dragon Slayer and Me

"You can only do something for the first time once," Melissa said with emphasis. Her comment in the shoe room that day reminded me of something Yogi Berra, the great Yankee catcher, might have said. I doubted Melissa was aware of Yogi, but she had a way of making statements so simple I had to shake my head, stop and think. I knew where this conversation was headed.

My trip to Cuba and the Boston Marathon bombing had exposed me to dance in a societal context. In Cuba, I had watched people dance, have fun, and express their unfiltered feelings to friends, strangers, and the community around them. After the marathon bombing, I watched the power of music and dance bring a dance tribe together and ease the pain of violence. I was learning to express my own feelings in dance. Dance had challenged me to feel and not just think about the people around me; to grow as a person. I had witnessed the pain of poverty in Cuba and the anger in Boston, yet the positive emotions that music and dance created in both cases overcame the dark side of life. Like a child learning a language, I was still awkward at communicating my own feelings in dance, but I would get better.

Both inside and outside the dance community people had many questions about Cuba, none more than Melissa. I let her inside my head and shared my thoughts about expressing my emotions more accurately and openly in dance. I mentioned visiting Ernest Hemingway's house in Cuba, recalling his books that I had read when I was younger and how he portrayed his male lead characters. Hemingway's men were usually strong, independent, and, like Hemingway, the man and the myth, could hunt and slay big game, fight in wars, drink all night, and persevere through adversity. But emotionally Hemingway's male characters were often underdeveloped; they kept their true feelings frozen, at least on the surface. Like Hemingway's characters, I had been raised at a time and in a culture where it was often important for men to control and hide their own true emotions. Dance avoidance fit my profile. There were times, looking back, though, when I knew avoidance was not honest. I now wanted to feel like the people I watched on the dance floor. I wanted to change.

My efforts at describing in words my quest for the feel of the dance to Melissa and Christine were imprecise at times. The problem was that the arrival and departure of the feel of the dance within me was unpredictable. When I first explained my experience on the white cloud they did not laugh, they understood. They just wanted more insight so they could help.

In the shoe room, I listened to Melissa and she recapped the benefits of attending Dance-O-Rama as I played the skeptic. All her points were pluses, but they did not move me to say yes. I agreed with her that first-time experiences are full of surprises and how we deal with them defines how we grow as people. I accepted her view that competing on a big stage would be a learning experience and build my confidence. We both agreed that Dance-O-Rama, or DOR, as I came to call it, could get me closer to the feel of the dance. The one thing Melissa did not mention was the dragon. Perhaps she thought the dragon was the reason I would not go? Ironically, this was the main reason I had to go to Washington. It was my opportunity to face the Dance Dragon, slay him, and free myself.

Melissa's success as a dance instructor was not defined by her ability to teach wedding people how to dance. That is easy for most instructors. Far harder is convincing a male student to attend DOR and perform a solo. Melissa believed that dancing helps people grow and have fun in the process. It is that belief that makes her convincing.

I listened to Melissa's pitch carefully that afternoon. She reminded me that I had grown as a person through dance. I reminded myself that

Melissa had helped make that happen. When I doubted my ability to learn to dance after twelve lessons, she'd convinced me to keep trying. When I danced the tango at a performance at the studio many months ago, she'd helped me prepare to face my dragon. Melissa had the skills to help men possessed by dance dragons; she was rare and so were my opportunities to defeat the dragon. Whether she knew it or not, Melissa was a dragon-slayer. If I wanted someone to drive the dragon out of my head, Melissa was the most qualified person I knew, and Dance-O-Rama was the place to do it. I told Melissa at the end of our conversation I was leaning toward committing, but I needed to talk things over with Eileen.

Later that evening, I mentioned to Eileen that we had a choice to make. For the same cost, we could go on vacation for a long weekend, relax, eat great food, and visit some art museums, or I could go to Washington, perform my solo, and she could watch. We agreed both to go to Washington, and that I had lost my mind.

In ballroom, there are two distinct activities for students: social dancing, and performance or competitive dancing. Most of my focus had been on social dancing. Male social dancers attend dance parties, go to clubs, and have a great time at weddings. The pressure to dance well socially depends on the real or imagined expectations and reactions of your dance partners. In performance, the outcome depends on the reaction of an audience and the judges. Most male students are social dancers and seldom chose to do solo performances; the self -imposed pressure that comes with performance, and being the leader, are two reasons why.

I had chosen to do my tango performance at the studio to put pressure on myself to learn to lead my dance partner. However, there is a big difference between doing a solo at your home studio and doing it at a major East Coast competitive event where the crowd was ten times larger and the level of dancing much higher. Male students who performed at a DOR events in the past sent me mixed messages. Some said it was a good way to learn and build confidence. Others said they only did it because they were under the influence of a charming instructor and said yes in a moment of temporary insanity. They would never do it again. No man I spoke to ever mentioned they competed at a

Dance-O-Rama event to slay a dragon. I was the lone man, along with three women, from our studio to commit that year, and by far the least experienced dancer.

Aside from all the student activities, on the final evening of Dance-O-Rama, the professional instructors competed. Melissa told me that those performances were always impressive to watch. What Melissa didn't tell me, until we arrived in Washington, was that she and her professional partner, Harrison, were competing there for the first time too. Washington would be a challenge for both of us, something Melissa could only do once as well. I found irony in the fact that Melissa and I would both be first-timers, albeit in different categories.

Amateur competition at DOR consisted of a series of mini-performances with four or five couples on the floor at the same time. Participants competed with dancers at their level and received grades and feedback from the judges. I would do a total of forty-two mini performances across a variety of dances and levels, plus a solo. The solo would take ninety seconds. We would have the entire ballroom floor to ourselves, with the judges', and all other, eyeballs in the audience focused on us. The Dance Dragon would most likely make his move then. If he won, and I had a meltdown on the floor, I was prepared to say that I gave dance my best effort, put my dance shoes away, and move on with life. If I succeeded and got past the Dance Dragon, then I would be free to pursue the feel of the dance.

I knew the key to my success was to practice relentlessly beforehand, focus one hundred percent during the dance, and always remember my goal—to defeat the Dance Dragon. The best way I explained my approach to my male friends was to compare it to golf. John Fitzgerald, a friend for thirty-plus years from my New York advertising days, lived on a golf course in North Carolina. John was not a ballroom dancer but, in the world of golf, I would describe John as a "mad one. " He loved the game, played nearly two hundred rounds a year, liked to walk the course, carry his own bag, and had a low single-digit handicap. If John were not so happy playing golf most days, he could teach it.

One week after I committed to perform, John and I played golf. He asked me numerous questions about dance, why I'd committed to DOR, and how I would prepare. On the second hole, John made a difficult shot from the rough on the edge of the green look easy. His ball landed five feet from the hole. When I complimented him, he smiled and mentioned he had practiced that shot a hundred times over the last year. I didn't need a calculator to realize John had hit an estimated ten thousand golf balls from the rough to improve just one aspect of his golf short game. For John Fitzgerald, practice was when he did his work; playing the game was his reward. I told him I wanted to take a similar approach to practice. But, unlike golf, dance practice often required a partner.

Golf and dance were also similar when it came to focus. The golfer had to focus one hundred percent on the ball, yet relax his body and grip and visualize in his mind the ball's direction and distance. In dance, I needed to relax my body, connect with my partner, and visualize my direction and pace on the floor. One difference between golf and dance was that, in golf, good etiquette required no conversation when another golfer was focused on hitting the ball. In dance, light conversation was often part of the experience. The reason was that the dancing couple needed to project the sense that they were enjoying themselves. In competitive golf, no one cared about the expression on your face or whether you were enjoying the company of other golfers. Conversation in dance can be an impediment to focus.

The second difference was that when I screwed up in dance, I needed to keep dancing because the music didn't stop until the end. In golf, there was a significant pause between each stroke. When you lost your focus in dance, you had to find a way to regain it in real time. John asked me how it felt to screw up on the dance floor. I told him the secret was not to let anyone, even yourself, know how you felt, and to act as if you hadn't made a mistake, to keep moving and smile even if you were truly mad at yourself.

As we played, John and I talked about motivation, attitude, and positive self-talk regardless of what was happening around you. We had run our first marathon together on a cold, wet night in Paris. The course was littered with runners who had stopped, many with cramps. For first-timers like us, that was not an encouraging sight. During our months of training, we had never discussed the possibility that we might have to stop. We had trained all winter long and traveled 3,500 miles to run. It was not likely we would have a second chance to run the Paris marathon. If I had known Melissa at the time, surely, she would have reminded me that you only experience the first time once. John and I both did a lot of positive self-talk that night, and finished the marathon.

Later in the round, I hit a five-iron shot off to the right. John identified my mistake as a fast swing. The tempo of my swing was off for some reason. He suggested, light-heartedly, that I slow down my swing, relax, and enjoy the moment. That I should think about music and then just let my body flow. While John had never met Melissa, he was beginning to sound like her. He went so far as to suggest that I use waltz timing and count I, 2, 3, as I started my swing back and 4, 5, 6 as I came down. It was good advice. My game improved. John surprised me. I told him he should take up dance, but he declined.

Melissa and I started practicing our solo four months before Washington. Melissa had familiarized me with the mini-dances we would be performing, so in lessons we went back and forth between the minis and the solo. I was happy with the amount of time I was practicing with Melissa and others. As for positive self-talk I decided to look in the mirror more often and say good things about myself. I found it humorous, but it kept my attitude centered.

On the dance floor, my biggest concern continued to be staying focused on the dance and the music. The more I thought about anything else, the less likely my body would be to surrender to the music. In rehearsal, sometimes I thought about past mistakes, my posture or my partner. For DOR dances, and particularly my solo, I needed to delete all that dance baggage from my head.

Two months before DOR, I developed tendonitis in my left Achilles tendon. At first, I tried to dance through the pain, but there were days when I favored my left foot significantly. I realized that it took two good feet to dance. I went to my doctor of thirty years. After he recovered from the initial shock of my new obsession, he asked me a dozen questions and was not surprised about my injury. I had witnessed people tear their Achilles on the squash court so we both knew what was at risk.

I went to see a physical therapist the same day. We started a program of stretching exercises, massages, and lots of ice. There is no simple explanation as to how a person gets tendonitis or how long it takes to clear up. Every day, I tried different combinations of ice, stretching the tendon, and taking Advil or Aleve. I stayed off my feet for a few days each week, with little walking and no dancing, to see if that would have an impact. After a month of treatments and sporadic dancing, no significant progress was made.

My body and the people around me sent different messages as to whether I should go to Washington. Eileen, who observed me daily, thought I should not go. She did not want me to develop chronic tendonitis or tear my Achilles. I talked to my physical therapist. She thought improvement would come in time provided I stuck with my treatment. I read everything I could about the Achilles. I asked my daughter-in-law, Erin, a physical therapist, for advice and she sent me some aggressive exercises to follow. My physical therapist in Boston kept pushing me and helped me strengthen my calf as well as my tendon. Two weeks before DOR, I sat down with her and asked for a go or no-go opinion. She said go. I was happy. She thought my tendon and surrounding muscles were now strong enough for dance, but that it might be painful at times. I had another choice to make. I could go to Washington, dance with some pain, and defeat the Dance Dragon, or change my plans and take a vacation.

By chance, my recent interest in Hemingway had me reading *The Old Man and the Sea*. Ernest Hemingway had a great grasp of human nature and men. The fact that I had visited his home in Cuba, as well as his favorite bar, rekindled my fascination with him. Hemingway loved nature, sports, a good drink, and female companionship, all of which made him a character in the public eye. I read about the old fisherman again and his epic struggle with the big fish. The old man's left hand had cramped up so much he could not open it. He practiced self-talk and told his left hand he would not allow it to prevent him from catching the fish.

The struggle of the old man on that boat typified the everyday struggles we face. The old man *had* to bring in that fish. I *had* to go to Washington to defeat the dragon. It was that simple and I was not going to let my Achilles get in my way. I would be diligent about doing my therapy. I would get comfortable with the pain. I even planned to talk to my Achilles, like the old man spoke to his left hand, and say positive things to it from time to time. The old man in the boat was determined to play the game out. His story gave me an extra push.

Chapter Eighteen

The Onesie Battle

On a cold December morning Eileen and I found ourselves at Logan Airport. I was ready for the trip to Washington D. C. I had practiced for months and, while the tendonitis was a nuisance, I erased it from my mind. I saw participation in DOR as the equivalent of final exams. But, unlike school, the only grade that mattered was the one I would give myself. The judges didn't know, nor could they ever understand, how I felt about my dancing. They could grade me on steps, posture, leading, and style, but only I would know if the Dance Dragon was defeated.

The event required a big suitcase. We would be dancing for three days. Women needed multiple dresses, skirts, shoes, jewelry, hair spray, and lots of fishnet stockings. Men had it much easier. My clothes were mostly black and my primary needs were white and black shirts, dance vests, a tuxedo, bow ties, and cufflinks. As the day wore on at such an event, some dancers would begin to sweat profusely, so back-up clothes were important. The goal was to plan well and eliminate any stress off the dance floor.

I traveled to the Gaylord National complex just outside Washington D. C. with three instructors—Kristen, Melissa and Fran - and three accomplished young female students - Pam, Andrea, and Karli. Of the female students, Karli was the one with whom I had most frequently danced. The previous summer, I had reluctantly agreed to participate in a choreographed team cha-cha group performance. It was a way to force myself to learn the dance. Everyone in the cha-cha group was a far better dancer than me. While it was frustrating, Karli made it bearable. She had a great temperament and practiced with me on the side. When the team performance was over, I admitted to Melissa that it had been a good learning experience. From her perspective, my momentary embarrassment was a small price to pay for the progress I made on the dance floor. Dragon-slayers can practice tough love at times.

At lunch, we talked about the low-key costume-party dance planned for that evening. No one talked about his or her upcoming performances. I sensed it was considered bad luck. Eileen and I listened to the chatter and ordered a beer with our lunch. Everyone else abstained. The centerpiece of Gaylord was an eighteen-story atrium that housed a very large Christmas tree and drew considerable interest during the holiday season. However, the primary location of interest to me was the large dance floor. It was intimidating and I needed to become comfortable with it.

Kristen seemed determined to distract the students from their performances by focusing on the costume party that evening. Kristen reminded me that I was going to be dressed as a big white tooth; most everyone else from the studio would be an elf. I drank my beer and nodded. Kristen had for weeks been sending emails to all of us to get buy-in on our collective costumes to the party that evening. I could not believe that I had agreed to dress up as a white tooth. I wondered whether I had lost my mind, or was just having a very weird dream. I had not paid much attention to Kristen's emails. My mind was focused on my solo and the Dance Dragon.

Costume parties were not new to the group. There were lots of theme parties at the Boston studio and most of us used our creativity and tried to participate. Usually the roles I chose to play were not that much of a stretch. I could have been a soldier, a baseball player, or a super-hero. Somehow, back in Boston, I had let my guard down and told Kristen she could design the white tooth-like prop. The good news was that no one I had ever met in my pre-dance lifetime would be at this event except Eileen. There was of course the potential risk that someone might have a camera or a video, and I could end up on the Internet. Oddly enough, that afternoon I was relaxed about the costume party. I realized that it might have seemed ridiculous to me a year ago, but nowadays wearing weird outfits and attending costume parties was becoming ordinary.

After lunch, as we walked back to the Gaylord, Melissa suggested I enjoy the fresh air as it would probably be the last time we would be outside for a few days. Melissa's comment sounded like something a prison guard would tell a new inmate. She was signaling that there was no escape. We were on the Potomac River, in the middle of nowhere, and I didn't have a car. My dance solo with Melissa was scheduled. I was in countdown mode for my own self-elected battle with the dragon. It would be part of the entertainment for the audience. When Eileen and I arrived downstairs outside the ballroom that evening, hundreds of people were gathered and dressed in colorful holiday costumes. The pressure switch was off and the mood was festive. Costumes alter our identity for a few hours, make for social conversation and create opportunities for people to meet.

Before I became a ballroom dancer, I would have labeled costume parties as silly. Now I did my best to participate and not prejudge the experience. At the studio, Eileen was more ambivalent in her approach. Some days, she would wear a costume and participate and other days she would forego the costumes. She objected to the time and effort required to identify a costume and the risk of looking like a fool. That night, Eileen came as an event spectator, not a participant, so she had a free pass on the costume party. She was looking forward to enjoying a holiday dance. We had a good time and the party was over at ten that night.

I woke up at 4:30 Friday morning and thought through my day. I needed to wear multiple outfits. I thought about the seven Ps that had been branded into my memory in the military, and had never left: *Proper Prior Planning Prevents Piss Poor Performance.* I did some stretching exercises before facing the dreaded task of putting on my onesie dress shirt. I would wear a white onesie tux shirt and a blue bowtie to complement Melissa's dress for the smooth dances and a tight-fitting black onesie shirt, and long black tie to match her black gown for the rhythm dances. My black formal dance pants were designed to highlight the posture of a male with straight uninterrupted lines from the ankle to the waist. Pants with pockets and baggy shirts and underwear were discouraged at performances. With no pockets in my formal dance pants, any money, credit cards, mints, gum, or lip balm would be spread inside my socks. Because I had once traveled so much, in both my military and then business lives, I had developed a life-long habit of using my socks as a place to carry valuables.

If you have changed a diaper, you know what a onesie is. They have snap-on buttons that hold the diaper tight around the crotch. Because they are one piece from the crotch up, a male adult onesie shirt will not bunch up or wrinkle, assuming it is the right size. Several of the female instructors and male dancers whose advice I trust suggested I purchase both a white and a black onesie shirt to avoid the bunched-up look that happens with shirts during a full day of dancing. What they forgot to tell me was to make sure I purchased a onesie with buttons around the crotch. Unfortunately, the white shirt I had purchased through the mail had none. A onesie with snap-on buttons for an adult male is easy to get into, but a onesie without the buttons over the crotch is a whole different story. Unlike infants, men lack the flexibility in their legs, hips, and shoulders to wiggle their way into a very tight onesie shirt without ripping it. Plus, infants are dressed by an adult. There was no way I was going to ask for help getting into my onesie.

I had practiced getting into the shirt twice before Washington, and early on discovered I could not do it standing up. Through trial and error, I had learned the best approach was to lie on the floor and pull the shirt up my legs much like underpants. My strategy was then to slowly twist and turn my arms and shoulders in spurts into the sleeves while I kept the rest of my body flat on the floor and held my core. I visualized medieval knights dressing for battle and considered myself lucky. I allocated twenty minutes for the effort that morning and was successful. Once the shirt was on, I banished any thought of the bathroom from my mind.

The remainder of my dressing went as planned. I looked in the mirror, practiced self-talk and complimented myself. When I arrived downstairs, I sat down at the table next to Fran and Karli, who were finishing breakfast. Their faces said they were taking the day seriously. Karli was all business and, I soon discovered, far more competitive than her laid-back disposition implied. My first dance was not scheduled until 9:20, so I had some time to practice with Melissa. Everything at Dance-o-Rama had been planned to the minute. I reminded myself that

I needed to appear relaxed even if I was not, make the dance look easy, and be a gentleman. I would not tolerate frustration in my head, let alone show it. I thought my expectations were reasonable. However, with more than forty dances over two days, I knew I would need a consistency of effort that I had never achieved before on the dance floor.

Melissa arrived, wearing her dance jacket over her dress to keep her warm. She asked me if I was ready for some practice dances. I was not surprised. I was happy she asked. Most of my adult life, I was at work at 8:30 in the morning, but today I was doing something that two years earlier was unimaginable. I was in a huge empty ballroom dancing the waltz to the song *Take it to the Limit*.

I was full of energy, maybe too much energy, and anxious for the competition to start. I looked at Melissa wondering if she might ask what I was thinking. My answer would have been "everything. " I doubted I could put all my thoughts and feelings into words.

As we practiced, I tried to focus and slow down my brain. I concentrated on the music as we did a waltz and remembered that it had once been painful to dance. That morning, dancing the waltz was a moment of pleasure. I could hear the beat, my posture was great, and the dancing "felt" good. I told myself that I had done all my homework and would have a great day. We then danced a foxtrot. I referred to the foxtrot as the happy dance. The reason was that compared to the other two smooth dances—the waltz and tango - the mood that foxtrot music created was often upbeat and cheerful. I felt more comfortable doing it than any other dance and, for that reason, it was the best dance for me to practice my smile.

Melissa was always on my case to smile. She thought I was too serious when I danced. A few weeks before DOR, she suggested I try telling her jokes, which would cause her to smile or laugh, and I would smile back. At least that was the theory. Days before going to Washington, I Googled dance jokes on the Internet. I looked for short jokes that were easy to remember and could be told with the beat of the music. I tried telling a joke that morning as we practiced the foxtrot. The joke didn't work. Rather than create laughter, there was confusion in Melissa's eyes. Joke-telling had never been my strength. I would have to develop another approach.

Next, we did a tango. I needed to project a different personality or mood from the foxtrot. My face showed no emotion. I looked away from Melissa as I bent my knees and led with my left heel as I moved across the floor. I was good at not smiling, but projecting fierceness when dancing was beyond me. As a tango dancer, I was still unpredictable. Some days I felt the music and stepped to the beat on time, and other days I did not. That morning I felt light and relaxed while I danced. My adrenaline was flowing and the Dance Dragon was in a deep sleep.

At 9:20 A. M. , Melissa and I walked onto the dance floor. I turned my back to the judges so they could read my number. I surveyed the floor and the four other couples who were in our heat. I looked at the table of people from my studio. I took a few deep breaths, repeated the word "relax" to myself multiple times, checked my posture, and calmly put my left hand out so Melissa could approach. I wondered whether she had Dance-O-Rama in her mind for me the first day I walked into the studio?Melissa had accomplished what people who knew me would say was impossible. I was impressed. It was time for her to enjoy herself. She had convinced me to keep dancing and given me the tools to fight the dragon. She had done her job.

Melissa and I danced the waltz, foxtrot, and tango three times each in the first thirty minutes. Each individual dance took about one minute and twenty seconds. The time flew by, and the details were a blur. I would not find out my scores until the next day. I was experienced enough to know what I did right and what I did wrong. One of the things I did right was not to show frustration when I made a mistake on the floor. I kept going. I did not frown or roll my eyes or mumble four-letter words, and that was important to me. It meant I was learning not to bring attention to my mistakes.

I ignored the people around me and managed a few smiles. Once or twice I made very subtle groans of dissatisfaction without moving my lips. I was not sure if Melissa had heard them. Melissa on occasion sent me messages with her fingers to keep me on beat. She also moved her head up ever so slightly if my head started to tilt forward. I briefly thought about the dragon that morning between dances. I assumed he was waiting for the right opportunity. No doubt the dragon saw my solo as his best opportunity to destroy the confidence I had worked so hard to build over the last six months.

Mid-morning, when we left the dance floor for another break, I remembered the night I tried to escape from dancingat the studio and Melissa stopped me. I smiled inwardly to myself. Progress on the dance floor defines itself in strange ways. The days of wanting to escape from the dance floor were behind me.

After the smooth dances, we had an hour to prepare for the four rhythm dances—the rumba, cha-cha, meringue, and triple swing. There was less floor-traveling in those dances. They required small, crisp steps, leading with the toe and the ball of the foot and pushing the feet down into the floor. Melissa did not waste any time. We used the hour and practiced. Melissa talked me through each dance and reminded me multiple times to slow down, bend my knees, push my feet into the floor, and enjoy. As we warmed up, there were times that I could feel the rhythm of the music with her and sometimes through her. The more we worked together, the more relaxed and confident I became.

My insurance policy that morning was Melissa. I think the Dance Dragon knew that as well. Confidence in my dance partner gave me more courage to try and find myself. As I did that, I became more independent in my dance. Dancing worked that way. Melissa had many non-verbal ways of communicating, and I had become good at recognizing them. At times, I felt as if we were playing charades. As the morning progressed, she needed to communicate less. The one constant was her eyes, which kept telling me to relax and enjoy. In theory, I was the leader on the dance floor and Melissa the follower; in reality,we were partners. Female partners can back-lead and most instructors are good and subtle at doing this. If we were too close to another couple on the floor, Melissa would find a way to take over without making it obvious.

We participated in twelve rhythm-dance performances, starting with several meringues, and then we danced a cha-cha to *Smooth* by Santana. For the swing dance, we danced to *The Wanderer* by Dion and *Rumor* by Adele. I learned the next day that I did reasonably well in most of these heats, the exception being the swing. In that dance, I struggled with the timing of the triple step and was uncomfortable with my body movement. I had no feel for the swing, even though I liked the music.

Something happened to me that day. I became a better dancer. My body and mind seemed in sync. The Dance Dragon was absent from my head. I was not tense and my passion for learning and improvement kept growing. I was even comfortable in my onesie. I was gaining confidence for my solo.

Chapter Nineteen

The Invisible Man

The five women at my table talked as if I wasn't there. After our afternoon dances, I did not need to be back on the dance floor until nine that night. I watched Karli, Pam, and Andrea practice their dances with Fran, chat among themselves and consult with Melissa and Kristen about all things related to feminine appearance. I never had the desire for a seat in the ladies' dressing room but that afternoon I imagined I was there. I listened to conversations on hair preparation, eye make-up, tanning spray, appropriate thigh, leg, and breast exposure, padding requirements, jewelry adjustments, and fingernail and toenail presentation. Female body parts, from the hair on their head down to their toes, were tools optimized for performance. I considered sharing my onesie experience but, compared to their efforts, my dressing experience was easy. As the day went on, I watched the women make slight modifications to their appearance as their performance time approached. I realized how naïve I was about women and performance dancing. I thought women only worked this hard getting dressed on their wedding day.

I smiled to myself as I considered the men who someday would encounter these young, disciplined, and motivated women. They had mastered the art of presentation, style, and glamour that ballroom dance performance required. The same skills were relevant off the dance floor. In rural Cuba, I watched dancers in everyday situations captivate an audience with their body movement, eye contact, passion, and spontaneity. In Washington, I observed the long-term detailed planning that goes into dress and overall physical appearance in performance dancing. Back at the studio, Pam, Karli, and Andrea dressed casually and did social dancing at parties for fun. They danced with anyone who asked and were always gracious and supportive with male beginners. When I watched them at DOR they danced at a different level. They pushed themselves and sought perfection with their partner, always with a smile. Like marathon runners, they were silently competing against other dancers or themselves. That afternoon as I sat at the table, I realized ballroom dancing was far more competitive among amateur women than I had ever imagined. Performance dancing was not for wimps. The women who competed left nothing to chance. Everything was planned. They had practiced for months, their focus was incredible, and they expected one hundred percent commitment and effort from their dance partner.

I looked at Fran, their dance partner and instructor who, like me, had been silent as the women talked. In a few minutes, Fran would start a long series of dance performances scheduled so he could rotate among the three women. His role that afternoon was simple: to make his dance partner, whoever she might be, look like the best dancer on the floor. He would need to be at the top of his game. He'd had his first practice session that morning at 6:30 A.M, almost nine hours before, and there had been little down-time. Each woman needed not only practice time, but the total emotional support of their male dance partner and that takes time and sensitivity. Under pressure, both male and female students can easily become jealous of a dance instructor's time with another student. I had no idea how Fran had the mental, physical, and emotional stamina to prepare all three women for what they hoped would be the best performances of their lives. He was fortunate that the three female students were strong supporters of each other.

What impressed me most about the women I had met in ballroom was that the majority had busy lives off the dance floor. These three young women were no exception. Andrea was studying to become a dentist; Pam worked in biotech, and Karli had a day job as a teacher and was pursuing her M. B. A. at night. Their dance goals and expectations were higher than my own. They were accomplished dancers and I could see they felt the pressure and would deal with it. I wanted to learn from them. I tried to imagine the mindset of the three women at my table. Of course, I had never walked or danced in their shoes.

I surveyed the room. I realized at no time in my life had I been in a room with so many well-dressed, highly motivated, and discreetly competitive women. Women wanted to be noticed on the dance floor far more than their male counterparts. Karli, Pam, and Andrea were quite different from one another in terms of body frame, skin tone, hair color, and height. The cut, style, and color of their dresses were selected to complement their bodies, and further accentuated their differences. On the practice floor, I saw the strength and power of Karli, the elegance of Andrea, and the energy and athleticism of Pam. These women would stand out on the dance floor.

One mini-crisis occurred that afternoon during the competition. Karli and Fran were competing in a cha-cha heat and the more Karli danced, the higher her short skirt crept up her thighs. I had never heard the term "skirt-creep" until that afternoon, but I quickly grasped its meaning. Unfortunately, in ballroom, unlike some sport events, there are no time-outs for hair, garment or shoe adjustments. I was sitting next to Karli's mother, who had driven down from Baltimore to watch her daughter perform. When Karli returned to the table for a short break in the competition her mother got right to the point. Karli had been so focused on her dance that she was totally unaware of the problem. Without a quick correction before her next dance she would stand out for the wrong reason. Karli's first reaction was shock and surprise but that did not last long; she quickly focused on finding a solution before her next dance. Kristen, the most experienced dancer at the table, went to find scissors and tape and suggested that by putting two-sided sticky tape on Karli's thighs, the skirt material would stick to her body, and that would temporarily prevent skirt-creep.

Kristen convinced Karli that her solution would work. Karli had to focus only on her dance; she had to believe Kristen was right, trust her body, and perform. Karli Jones had been a competitive collegiate gymnast and her mental discipline showed when she returned to the floor. That afternoon, I had a lesson in focus. The next day, Karli was recognized as the top medal-winner in her category for her overall dance performance.

Friday at dinner, we gathered to relax, discuss the day's events, and prepare ourselves for a two-dance competition that evening in our respective divisions. My dance plan called for a rumba and a waltz. There were multiple heats and perhaps twenty-five couples at my level. The day's events had dramatically heightened my sensitivity to female wardrobes. At the dinner table, I was dressed in a tuxedo, seated next to my instructor. Melissa's appearance that evening and throughout our entire time in Washington was flawless. She was a beautiful young woman, built to dance, and dressed to augment her physical assets in an elegant way. I had learned much that day about the effort women make in dress and appearance. I was resolved, not only at dance events, but also in life, to notice and compliment such efforts.

After dinner, we returned to the ballroom. At nine that evening, almost twelve hours after my first dance competition that day, I was ready. Dancing for me had become energizing. The more I danced, the more I wanted to dance. I was happy that the urge was still strong. When our names were called, I walked onto the floor with Melissa and soaked in the environment. I noticed the other couples on the floor and distanced us from them. I turned my back for the judges, put my hand out for Melissa and smiled. Melissa had started dancing with me more than twelve hours before. I wondered whether she was still enjoying herself or looking for the day to end. Her face and body language said she was happy but she was a professional so I was unsure as to her state of mind. It made no sense to ask the question, as I knew what she would say. As we waltzed, there were a few moments when my mind turned off and my body took control. I connected to the music and floated on a cloud. The waltz that night had teased me with the feel of the dance. When I snapped out of it I laughed to myself and instinctively smiled at Melissa. She smiled back.

After the waltz, I put my hand out again for Melissa, smiled and invited her to dance the rumba. This time I held my smile for fifteen seconds. I was making progress on my smiles. As the rumba ended, I spun Melissa around, nodded my head in appreciation, and said "thank you for a wonderful day". I offered my right arm, as a gentleman would, and we walked off the floor together. That Friday was a very good day.

Chapter Twenty

Those Sweet Words

After a deep and dreamless sleep, I woke up early Saturday morning feeling great. I had no aches or pains, and whatever mistakes I'd made on the dance floor the day before had evaporated from my mind. I was focused only on this day. I would do twenty-one dances in open competition. The difference between "open" and "closed" competition is that the open category allows for some choreography and personal style. Later in the day, I would do my solo and then relax and begin to live the rest of my life.

For experienced dancers, the open category provided a dancer with the opportunity to move their body and express themselves creatively. Melissa had choreographed a few simple open moves for each dance. She was trying to build my confidence while at the same time avoid the possibility of a meltdown. We both knew my priority was our solo dance later that day. I wondered if the day would ever come when I would have the confidence, or, more importantly, the instinct, to just "let go" and be creative on the dance floor while leading my partner. Occasionally, when I was practicing by myself and no one was around, I just listened to the music, trusted myself and moved my entire body. However, I never did it in the presence of another person. If I was lucky, my mind might travel to that special place and set me free. The problem was, like waking up after a dream, I did not know how to return to that special place.

On the dance floor that Saturday morning, there was no tension in my body, no butterflies. I was immune to the audience and felt totally in sync with Melissa. Of course, only Melissa knew if we were in sync for sure. Occasionally I screwed up and then quickly got back on track. I did a great cha-cha, but I did not know why. Somehow in that one dance, everything came together. A good dance is comparable to sinking a 40- foot putt after missing a couple of easy six-footers earlier in the day. I guess that is part of the tease of ballroom dancing. I received a considerable amount of positive feedback from my female student teammates that morning. Peer feedback in dance is different from instructor feedback. It can be more honest and less informed, but both are usually well intentioned. In my endless search for informed and objective feedback, I discounted the positive feedback that instructors provided by at least 25 percent. However, even with the discount, I knew I was a better dancer on Saturday. There was a part of me that said I should be happy with how I performed that morning. Another part of me said, "be careful"; I had not yet performed my solo and that was the reason I came to Washington. I thought about the first time I saw the Dance Dragon's shadow in high school and then quickly put him out of my mind. I was starting to understand both the joy and the frustration of performance dancing in the ballroom world.

Waiting to perform unfortunately allowed me time to think. That too was part of the DOR experience. My morning dances concluded at 11:30 a. m., then I had three hours to wait until my solo, three long hours to think. Three hours to block the dragon out of my head. In football, in a close game, the outcome is often decided by a field goal. There is a tactic called "icing the kicker" where the opposing team calls time-out to disrupt the kicker. The idea is to give the kicker some time to think, in the hope that it may cause him to lose his rhythm and fail to kick the ball between the uprights. Waiting for a performance dance can result in over-thinking and, like the kicker, the leader can be off-rhythm as he starts the dance.

"I want to dance better. " That is what I'd said to myself after I completed my first tango solo performance at the studio. That night was a turning point in my dance life. The dance had been performed in front of a small and friendly crowd with hometown judges but neither the crowd or the judges were the point. The fact was I had held my ground against the Dance Dragon. It was a major step forward in my journey. However, in sports lingo that night was an exhibition game. After doing that tango, I started to consider doing something I swore I would never do—the real thing, a solo performance at a major competitive event. I needed to confront the Dance Dragon and demonstrate he no longer had any control over me. Only then, would I be free to pursue the feel of the dance.

My mind turned to butterfly management and the need to project self-confidence. Butterflies happened because embarrassment, often in the form of failure, was a threat to our ego. Butterflies might flutter in our stomach before we speak publicly, go on a first date, or walk on an athletic field for the first time. Butterflies are associated with a "fight or flight" response to a situation. The blood in our body moves from a place where it might not be temporarily needed, like our stomach, to our legs. This blood movement causes the flutter and, in more extreme cases, it can cause people to faint or feel nauseous.

I remembered the first morning I made a major presentation to a large business audience. I couldn't eat. After I arrived at the podium and started to speak, I couldn't stop my right leg from shaking. The butterflies had taken over. Flight was not an option; it would have cost me my job. The good news was that the podium hid my legs from the audience. In time, as I focused on the audience and kept taking deep breaths, the butterflies exhausted themselves and flew away. As the years went by, I became better at butterfly management. When they arrived, I told myself to ignore them and focus on the task at hand. If my first approach failed, I breathed in often and deeply and imagined the smell of ocean air and the sound of waves until a calm came over me. As I exhaled, I visualized the butterflies flying away.

Life without butterflies would be boring. We must risk embarrassment and failure to experience all that life offers. One of my goals in dancing was to reach the point where I would not turn down a request to dance. The irony in that goal was not only would I need to fight off butterflies, but I also had to accept the moments of frustration, embarrassment, and temporary failure that learning to dance required. There were no short cuts.

The music Melissa and I had selected for our solo routine was the Norah Jones song *Those Sweet Words*. I enjoyed listening to Norah Jones long before I started dancing. For some male beginners, the rumba was difficult because it required considerable knee and lower body movement. The rumba was an intimate dance of passion. The best rumba performance I had seen was the birthday dance in the Cuban mountains. The couple we watched were great dancers, but it was their honest expression of love for each other that made the dance memorable. In the rumba, partners stood close and faced each other, moved their bodies in sync, and looked directly into each other's eyes. At that point in my dance life, I was still learning to drive the car, so to speak, so expressing passion on the dance floor was a stretch. Initially during rumba practice for my solo when I looked in the mirror, I saw a serious frown on my face. I worked hard at eliminating the intense frown. I experimented with happy and romantic facial expressions and met with mixed results. Some days I wondered how Melissa or Eileen kept a straight face while dancing the rumba with me.

Thirty minutes before our performance, we did a dry run outside the ballroom on the lobby rug. I was indifferent to the people walking by, remaining focused on my dance, and listened to Melissa mingle light conversation with dance-step reminders. I sensed she was trying to get a read on my nerves without making me nervous. I tried to get a feel of my body. I was a bit shaky but could not figure out whether it was cold in the lobby or if the butterflies were getting ready to attack. After ten minutes, I was warm, felt more in control, and there wasn't a butterfly in sight.

In a mini-performance with four or five other couples on the floor, the individual judges spentseconds watching each couple dance before switching to another couple. In a solo, the judges and the audience watched the lone couple for the entire dance. The intensity of four-hundred-plus pairs of eyeballs watching me in a solo played on my mind. As the male, I was evaluated for my posture and frame throughout the dance, my ability to lead, and how well I kept pace with the beat. The judges and the audience were also reading the connection between my partner and myself, our facial expressions and our body language. The more we enjoyed each other's company, the better. There was a major skill and age gap between Melissa and myself, and that would draw the crowd's attention. Her dress, her movement, and everything else about her appearance caught people's eyes. That was the good news. The bad news was I still did not move my body or smile like a dancer.

Those Sweet Words is a song full of romance, passion and a hint of fun. Throughout our final rumba practice, Melissa reminded me to reflect that mood and always maintain eye contact with her. In social dancing, making and holding eye contact and smiling at an attractive lady in a relaxed environment while you danced are usually easy. However, the intensity of focus I needed in a choreographed performance made eye contact and smiling very difficult for me.

Our warm-up on the rug ended. The performances began in ten minutes. I asked Melissa if they had locked the ballroom doors. I got a great smile from her and realized I should have saved that question until we were on the dance floor. Melissa and I stood by the team table and watched the other couples perform. Occasionally Melissa would reach out for my hand and we moved our feet in place to whatever music played. Movement kept us warm and relaxed. I was past the point where I could prepare. My fate had been decided. I just wanted to dance, get this performance behind me and destroy the Dance Dragon.

As the clock ticked, I tried to think of something other than dance. My mind drifted to the ocean again. It was a warm summer day in my youth, and I was standing alone on a large rock. I was debating with myself whether I should jump into the cold waters of the North Atlantic and join my three friends. The swim from the rocks to the shore at high tide had become a rite of passage for teenage boys. I decided to stop thinking about the cold water and the distance and jumped. After the shock of the cold water passed, I found my rhythm and my breath. I knew I was going to be the last one to reach the beach, but I was only interested in racing myself. I just needed to finish the longest swim of my young life.

Our names were called, and I extended my right arm to Melissa, held my head up, and escorted her to the middle of the dance floor. I took a few deep breaths and exhaled slowly. I focused on Melissa's eyes and blocked out everything else while I waited for Norah Jones' voice and the music to *Those Sweet Words*:

What did you say
I know I saw you saying it
My ears won't stop ringing
Long enough to hear
Those sweet words
What did you say?

I invited Melissa to join me in dance with my left arm, and she moved close to me. I closed my right arm around her and placed my right hand on her shoulder blade. My mind was thinking in slow motion while my body moved in real time. The dance began. We did a basic rumba box, and I counted the beat to myself to relax and capture the rhythm in my body. Melissa smiled and her blue eyes sparkled about a foot from my face. I tried to reciprocate with a smile but Melissa was a performer, while I had the confused mind of a novice dancer. My face could not execute what my brain requested. Smiles come to me when I'm happy, stress-free, and my facial muscles are relaxed. At that moment on the dance floor, my face could not hide the truth; it was frozen with tension.

I gave up my efforts to fake a smile, as it was not my top priority. I needed to focus on my routine. We danced through some crossovers and then a cross-body lead. I told myself that the day would come when I would enjoy the rumba, and put some style, personality, and a smile into my performance, but today was not that day. Today was simply about survival and getting through my performance. It was about defeating the Dance Dragon.

I stepped back and raised my left arm, Melissa turned 180 degrees as we kept moving our feet to the beat. Melissa was now facing the audience, and I was dancing in shadow to the left and right behind her. I held her hands over her shoulders as we moved side to side. Melissa glanced over her left shoulder and gave me another smile. I laughed a bit and for a few seconds I was enjoying myself. All eyes were on Melissa as I led her, and her ability to connect with the audience provided me with a few moments to relax. I was more than halfway through the routine when I reminded myself to hold my head up and lean slightly forward while I kept my back straight. We did some Cuban walks as we moved across the floor and swayed to the music. I felt some tension grow within me as I prepared to dip Melissa. We came together and I moved my left foot to the side and led my partner into a back dip over my knee. We then stood up straight, smiled at each other, bowed to the audience, and started walking off the floor.

I took several deep breaths as I walked and literally blew the air out of my lungs. At least that is what I think happened. Parts of the dance had been a blur. I had performed my solo, and now I just wanted to disappear. I wanted to unravel both my thoughts and feelings. I had done something I had never imagined doing in my lifetime. It felt good. The Dance Dragon in my head was silent, stunned in defeat. I could barely see him in my mind's eye. I looked at the dance floor and saw the shadow of a small, frail, and hunched-over dragon slowly fade away. I had won a battle that no else saw. I was free.

It is very hard to evaluate your own solo dance performance. I had to remind myself of my goal. Every dancer starts from a different place in terms of experience, talent, and managing their own expectations. As a newcomer performing a solo, my dance was not about perfection; it was about passage to another phase in my dance life. Ultimately, each student determines if the mental effort of a solo performance, as well as the time, money, and risk of embarrassment, is worth the benefit. In my case, I had chosen to do something that was clearly out of my comfort zone. I relied on a dragon-slayer to help prepare me. I had elected to confront my own fears. I was happy with the outcome.

Later that day, several friends who lived in the area and had known me for decades arrived. They asked what I'd learned from the experience. Performance dancing is a different game from social dancing, I replied. It requires that you commit to endless hours of practice and the pursuit of an unachievable goal, perfection, with a single partner who must have the same mindset. Unlike running a marathon or skiing a tough trail, the outcome of my first major competitive dance performance was not only up to me, it was up to both of us. It required that I dance with a partner who had far more experience and skill than myself. If I wanted to do well, I needed to place my fate in Melissa's hands, trust her and adapt to her leadership. Performance dancing also required that I adapt to the broader, more formal culture of ballroom.

For me that was not easy. The emphasis on dress, etiquette, good manners, tradition, and positive support was more female than I had experienced in life. Within the culture there was no place to hide. Honest feedback about dance feelings was a requirement, four-letter words were never used and praise was the focus of most conversations. If I had the power, there might be some aspects of ballroom culture I would change, but that was not my call. I needed to adapt to the culture, as it was if I wanted to succeed. When the experience was over I had felt a rush. I was pleased not just that I had finished the dance and defeated the dragon, but that I had done it within an environment that was out of my comfort zone.

My focus shifted to Melissa's upcoming performance in the professional competition. That evening she and her partner, Harrison would be performing professionally for the first time. They were a great couple on the dance floor, but how they would perform among other young professionals in their category was unknown. Harrison had arrived early that morning at breakfast after an overnight bus ride from Boston. He looked like he needed a nap, but I'm sure his mind was on his performance. While I had been taking lessons from Melissa for a long time, I knew her mostly in her role as instructor and was not qualified to evaluate Melissa the performer. Often at the studio, I had watched her dance. I found her inspiring, but I was her student and thus biased.

Late in the afternoon during a break in the performances, I had an opportunity to dance with Melissa. I felt the need to voice my support for her upcoming performance. At the same time, I wanted to respect her pre-performance game plan, which I presumed was not to think about it. There was a debate going on in my head as to when and what I should say. We had talked for the better part of two days about my own dancing, as that was Melissa's way. To ask Melissa questions about her own performance was to enter uncharted waters. She seldom talked about herself unless I asked her a direct question. Plus, I was clearly not in any position to offer her advice. A lull in our conversation occurred, and I decided to ask how she prepared herself for her performance. Her answer was brief and consistent with my expectations. She was trying not to think about it. I read from her eyes a quiet "thank you for asking" message. A conversation was not necessary. She had done everything she could to prepare herself. She was focused on her goal. Chitchat was not required from me; enough said.

My original plan that Saturday evening had been to leave DOR and spend the night on the town with my friends. However, over the previous few days I had thought about Melissa's performance and decided I needed to be present. This was a big night for my instructor and mutual support was part of ballroom dance culture. We had traveled a long distance in our dance life together. My friends understood my need. We enjoyed a cocktail and caught up on our collective lives. Then I returned to my room, changed into a tuxedo, and headed off to the closing award dinner and the professional dance competition. I found the studio table and sat next to Melissa. Kristen was seated on her other side. We exchanged table small talk but clearly there was tension in the air.

The main course for dinner that evening was a large filet mignon with gravy served over mashed potatoes with a side of carrots. Melissa sat there with her perfect posture and eyed the plate with indifference. Either she did not like gravy or she had no appetite. I suspected the latter. I sat there in silent support. I thought about baseball where the pitcher is often left alone on the bench between innings to ponder his game. I had never been to a major dance event where professionals compete so I was not sure as to what was good supportive behavior. I trusted my gut, which told me to avoid idle conversation.

During dinner, the amateur awards were presented. I received an award as a Top Student Newcomer within my age category. It was a small category, but recognition was part of the ballroom dance culture so I appreciated the well-intended gesture.

When the professional competition began, I was awestruck. I had never been to a live ballroom dance performance and here I was with a seat on the edge of the floor. The sheer energy of the tango dance competition blew me away. The female wardrobes were provocative and the level of dancing was beyond anything I had seen in person in my life. The performers came within inches of my face. I could hear them breathe and see the intensity in their eyes. As the dance continued, their posture and body frame never sagged, and I wondered how they ever developed such stamina and body control. It must have taken years of effort for an individual to earn a place on the dance floor with this group. These dancers lived to dance and it showed.

Melissa and Harrison were entered in the Rising Stars professional-level competition, and the expectation voiced at the table was that their best chance to win an award was within the "Smooth" category, which consisted of the tango, waltz and foxtrot. Melissa and Harrison, as a dance couple, would stand out on any dance floor. Melissa, in her dance shoes, is close to six feet tall, slender, with white skin, blue eyes, and light hair. Harrison is perhaps 6 feet 4 inches, with dark skin, a full, muscular body frame, and black hair. Their eyes and smiles told you they are very likeable people, and that was important to an audience. When their names were called to perform, our table erupted with support. I was a totally biased observer. When the music played, I watched Harrison and Melissa dance a waltz as close to the judges as possible. I thought that was a bold move. Suddenly there was a traffic jam and they simply stopped, danced in place, and waited before they continued. I thought their self-control was impressive, but I did not know what a judge would think. When the dance ended, their facial expressions said they were satisfied with their performance. They were happy and appeared quietly confident.

In a short time, Melissa and Harrison were announced as winners in the Smooth category. It made for cheerful faces not only at our table but also across the ballroom. This was their first time at a big event and their performance connected with the judges and audience. While it may have seemed clichéd, hard work paid off, and Melissa and Harrison had put in the effort. A few minutes later, I had the chance to congratulate the winners, and seeing the looks on their faces made being there in person quite special. Melissa's passion for dancing was the same as it was the first day I met her. Her smile was one hundred percent real. As the event continued, I stood next to Melissa and talked about her dancing and how special it was for me to see her perform. I wished everyone in the Boston studio could have been there. Saturday was another very good day in my dance life.

Later, Eileen and I talked about the evening. She had been out to dinner with our friends, as admission at the performance was limited to DOR participants. Eileen talked about her own passion for dance and wondered whether she too should perform at a future event. We talked about the way people got high on dancing. We joked about the song *Hotel California* by the Eagles and wondered whether it could be adapted to portray life in a dance studio. The lyrics, "You can check out anytime you want but you can never leave" stood out in our minds. Dance was hard to walk away from. I wondered about my own dance future and if I would ever want to "check out", or if I could ever leave.

Chapter Twenty-One

Joy, Struggle, and Freedom

I once saw ballroom dance as a form of self-inflicted pain that I should avoid. I had no clear idea of what it was, nor did I know anyone who did it. In my mind, ballroom was limited to the waltz, tango, foxtrot, and some form of European polka. A few high-school dance classes, old movies, and the early days of television shaped my perception. After I left Dance-O-Rama, I saw dance in a different way. Images of Fred Astaire, Elvis, Louis Armstrong, and Etta James, Sinatra, Michael Jackson, and many others were in my head along with the sounds of rock and roll, country and western, and Latin music. Ballroom dancing kept evolving due to the ever-changing popularity of music, the desire of people to move their bodies, and the emergence of new media.

My studio in Boston was located about a mile from my home and most evenings when I walked there and back, dancing was on my mind. My walk took me past a symbol of another time, the Puritan-era burial grounds on Boston Common. I thought about the ghosts of the people who had walked on the same path three centuries ago. Sometimes I stopped and listened to music on my iPhone. If the foot traffic was light on the path, I might find myself practicing a few dance steps or the Cuban motion. I looked at the gravestones and imagined how the people resting under those stones would respond to my behavior. How would they react to my dancing the triple swing to the song *Addicted to Love* by Robert Palmer or dancing the tango to *Kiss of Fire*? Would they feel joy and freedom, or would they see sex and sin? In some parts of the world, puritanical mores still exist. People are not allowed to express themselves through dance. I told myself as I stood there that I was lucky to live today in this place. I moved on, excited about going to my dance lesson.

I could never have imagined the people I met in my dance life. I needed to watch, listen, talk, dance, smile at them, and touch them to discover who they were and why they danced. To the outsider, as I once was, ballroom dancers first appeared weird and off-centered. Now, as a ballroom dancer myself, I saw honesty, passion, and kindness in dance. The differences in cultural backgrounds, skin color, size, gender, and age within my dance community were real, but they were irrelevant. What we shared is what mattered: a desire to learn and experience everything dance offers and a willingness to accept the struggle along with the joy, to be honest with ourselves and supportive of each other. When I think about ballroom culture now, I see much of the good that life provides.

The day I opened the door to the studio for the first time, which I could only do once, I had no idea that the journey would lead me to dance with more than 3,000 women, do a solo performance in Washington D. C. , or travel to the rural mountains of Cuba to experience the feel of the dance. My journey created a desire to connect not only with the dancers of the present but also, in some way, with those of the past. I learned that dances such as the waltz, the tango, and the rumba were a means by which people over the centuries sought to express themselves and give both joy and solace to another person or their community in good and bad times. I connected through the tango to Kapka Kassabova and her Bulgarian roots, her life in New Zealand and her travels to Buenos Aires, New York and Paris. I connected through the rumba and cha-cha to Africans placed in slavery, taken to Cuba and the Caribbean and comforted by music and dance. I connected through the waltz to the peasants of Europe, their weddings, celebrations and funerals. And I will forever be connected through the foxtrot and *Sweet Caroline* to the people of Boston and the marathon bombing.

People now ask me the same question I once asked everyone I met in ballroom: why do you dance? My answer remains the same, although the order of the three words may change depending on the day. Dance for me is about feeling the struggle, freedom, and joy that is life. On any given day when I dance, I honestly don't know which feeling will dominate my dance. I have learned dance mirrors life. When ballroom dancing is good, every aspect of my being is alive—I'm full of joy and energy, I'm free from everything around me, and I'm connected to all people present and past who cherish such moments. Those are the moments when I truly feel the dance. I couldn't explain it at the time, but it happened at my daughter's wedding, the studio in Boston after the Boston Marathon bombing, and under the stars in rural Cuba. The feel of the dance has also happened at family weddings, parties, dancing to *Take This Waltz* with Eileen, and during lessons with Melissa, Christine, and other instructors. The more I experience the feel of the dance, the more I understand it, and the more often I want to make it happen. Learning to dance did not come easy for me. I will never sugarcoat the challenge when asked. I knew the effort it took and the mindset I had to cultivate. I struggled often to hear the beat, move my body, fight my inhibitions, and connect with my partner. When my feel for the dance was weak, I felt frustrated and missed the joy, but I knew I would try again.

One night I was sitting outside the dance studio on a bench in a small city park drinking a smoothie that Jessica Bolster suggested I try. Jess had arrived at the studio shortly after me. We had grown up on the dance floor together. We were talking about dancing, our mutual struggles, and laughing about our inability to remember the names of the steps and the collisions we had experienced on the dance floor. I asked Jess if the frustration ever made her think ballroom dancing was not for her. She looked at me and said, "Dancing is probably the scariest thing I have tried to do in my life. As a beginner, it is very hard for me to walk into the studio every night. But life has taught me that if I'm not frustrated at times, then I'm probably not growing as a person. "

There is no quit in Jessica; she knew why she danced, and her words made me smile. We, like other students, chose to learn something that was very hard for us to do. We knew there would be moments of frustration. We knew we had to learn to "dance as if no one is watching. " We knew we had to learn to "feel the dance" like Lola and experience the "freedom" that Melissa the dancer and Maria the young Cuban woman enjoyed. We knew we had to strive to achieve "the complete joy of the dance experience" that Jonas described. I knew all this to be true because dancing with 3,000 women told me so.

Epilogue

Some mornings I practice a few dance steps at home while I look after my eighteen-month-old granddaughter. Bea's face is smeared with strawberry juice from the fresh berries she has been eating. She sits in her high chair while I dance a few feet away. I move my body to the music and Bea watches me intently. If I go off-beat, she gives me her inquisitive look and starts to move her body correctly to the beat until I adapt. With her body, she tells me to slow down and enjoy the moment. If I move my arms in and out to the music of the rumba, she will watch and then join me with the happy smile that only a child can provide. We feel the dance together.

Dance is now an integral part of my life. Looking back, I can say I was a fool for avoiding dance for most of my life, but guilt would not be consistent with the spirit of ballroom. It is better that I look forward. I have discovered dance and the joy people derive from the experience. Dance is an emotional language that enables us to communicate with each other and that transcends time and place. I can now share that experience, and I can support others who want to take the journey. Dancing, like watching the white clouds move across the sky or inhaling the smell of the ocean, is an integral part of the joy of life.

CPSIA information can be obtained
at www.ICGtesting.com
Printed in the USA
BVOW08s1331230717
489697BV00003B/265/P